Shambhala

Shambhala

The Road Less Travelled in Western Tibet

Laurence J. Brahm

Marshall Cavendish
Editions

All photographs by Dou Yan, Chief Cinematographer, Ji Xiaoming and
Laurence J. Brahm of Red Capital Studio

Published by Marshall Cavendish Editions
An imprint of Marshall Cavendish International (Asia) Private Limited
1 New Industrial Road, Singapore 536196

Other Marshall Cavendish Offices
Marshall Cavendish Ltd. 119 Wardour Street, London W1F 0UW, UK
• Marshall Cavendish Corporation. 99 White Plains Road, Tarrytown
NY 10591-9001, USA • Marshall Cavendish International (Thailand) Co
Ltd. 253 Asoke, 12th Flr, Sukhumvit 21 Road, Klongtoey Nua, Wattana,
Bangkok 10110, Thailand • Marshall Cavendish (Malaysia) Sdn Bhd, Times
Subang, Lot 46, Subang Hi-Tech Industrial Park, Batu Tiga, 40000 Shah
Alam, Selangor Darul Ehsan, Malaysia

Marshall Cavendish is a trademark of Times Publishing Limited

National Library Board Singapore Cataloguing in Publication Data

Brahm, Laurence J.
Shambhala / Laurence J. Brahm. – Singapore :
Marshall Cavendish Editions, 2006.
p. cm.
ISBN : 981261284X

1. Shangri-La (Imaginary place)
2. Lhasa (China) – Description   and travel.
3. Tibet (China) – Description and travel. I. Title.

DS785
951.5 -- dc22   SLS2006022143

ISBN-13: 978-981-261-284-7
ISBN-10: 981-261-284-X

Printed in China

Dedicated to
a Bodhisattva in disguise

The lover from whom I met and passed by chance,
Is a girl with a perfumed body.
It is like picking up a turquoise of whitish lustre,
And throwing it away off-hand.

If I reciprocate with the feelings of the girl,
My share in religion during this life will be deprived.
If I wander among the solitary mountain ranges,
It would be contradictory to the wishes of the girl.

~The Love Songs of the 6th Dalai Lama,
Tsangyang Gyatsho (1683-1706)

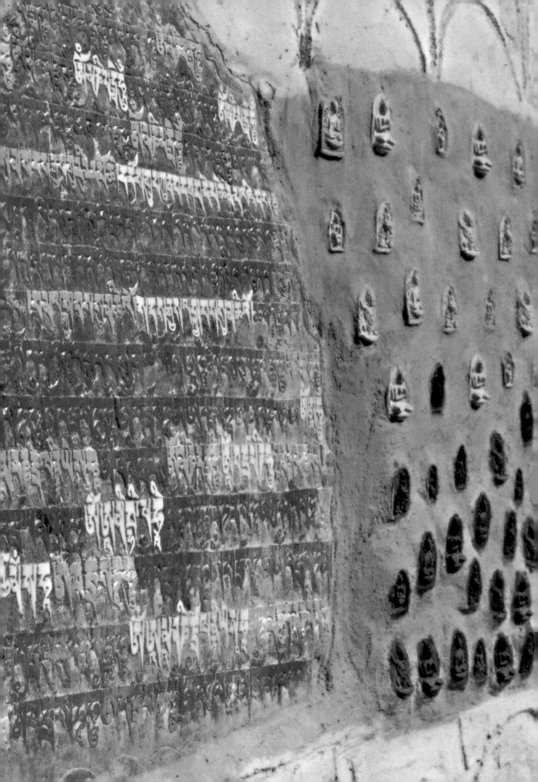

Contents

"A meditating person has one point of view, one traveling this world another view. There are many points of view. Which is true?

A person who travels the world looking for Shambhala cannot find it. But that does not mean it cannot be found."

Shambhala Sutra
The Sixth Panchen Lama
Losang Palden Yeshe (1737-1780)

Qinghai
NOMAD
Country
Yak!
Shambhala Sutsa says follow the clearest direction!
LHASA
Renzhendeki's Teahouse
TARA TEMPLE
Barkor
La Zha's ANTIQUE store
Chakpori Hill
Jokhang Monastery
Barkor
Beru khyentse Rimpoche's Home
Thimpu
Myanmar

Going

I had been here before. I remembered clearly. I tried to remember, but was just not sure. I tried to remember again.

I was four years old. It was a dream. I ventured into a canyon without time, a canyon spreading into desert, a space without perimeters. Directions became meaningless. The space stretched into eternity without form. Mountains dominated everywhere. On the horizon, they dissolved to dust. There was no sense of direction at all, and no reason to be. Creeping awareness whispered deep within me that there was no way to leave the desert except to cross it. Unable to return on the path entered, I awoke crying.

I was a teenager when the dream occurred again. Entering a dimensionless realm, the canyon reappeared. This time it was narrower and deeper but quickly spread into desert. I could not find my way across the desert. The mountains ahead felt threatening, almost surreal in the power they exuded. To reach the mountains, I suspected, this desert would have to be crossed. I was certain it could not be crossed. If the desert could not be crossed, this place must be an illusion. Concern became fear. It struck like darkness, warning me to leave immediately. This time, I did not cry but quickly backtracked the path I took. Within moments, I was awake in my dark bedroom in Connecticut. A full moon bathed the lawn outside. Autumn leaves scattered.

I was a university student when the dream occurred a third time. The canyon reappeared, floating in mist. There were lush plants growing in cracks of sulfite spitting rocks. It had just rained and dew was quickly bringing life out from dust. Thunder echoed somewhere else. It faded from this place, and was no longer present. Wind blew, creeping across my shirt. Dust scattered, then eroded. Plateaus cracked. They became canyons. Rain froze. It became snow. Wind coughed. Snows blew in six directions. Suddenly, the desert was covered by vast blanketing snows. Stone cliffs stared down white. They too were covered with snows. Soon, it all began to drift.

I knew that passages would be blocked and began to leave quickly. There was only one passage, a thin gravel road, distinct because it was so bare. The place entered was the only way to leave. If I did not leave quickly, I knew it would soon be blocked by snow. Afraid of this place, I left, awakening in a student dorm. Beer cans were strewn all over the campus lawn, bathed in blue autumn moonlight outside my window. They were covered in dew. It was early morning. Breathing deeply, I had awoken.

The last time this dream occurred, I was a lawyer working for a prestigious international law firm in Hong Kong. The excitement of professional life had become a labyrinth of stress. There seemed to be no exit except vacations in Phuket resorts where I ran into the same clients I wanted to escape from. Political infighting between partners in the law firm seemed to dwarf the United Nations. I took airplanes more frequently than public buses. I no longer had time to feed my dog.

After almost daily evening networking cocktail parties, I worked through each night to finish contracts for clients, so I could go to the fitness center and squeeze in a workout before returning to the office where I usually spent the night. I began to miss my workouts and stayed at the computer all night writing documents until I fell asleep at my desk in the early awakening hours. It was on just such a night the dream came back.

This time, canyon erupted like hell. I fell into the desert and landed on a sand dune. The wind blew and sand covered me. I wiped it from my eyes and looked around. The desert expanded in all directions. There were bones of carcasses with dried meat and patches of fur hanging from their rib cages. Black ravens feasted. Skulls of what seemed like large cows were stacked on piles of rocks. The ravens tore meat from the skulls. The sun was a distinct orange. The sky was turquoise blue. And the desert expanded into pools of waters, lakes that could not be crossed because the alkaline was so concentrated they were poison. Beyond the desert were mountains. They could not be crossed either because their passes were blocked, smothered in snow. Beyond the mountains there was another desert. I was not quite sure what was to be found in that other desert beyond the mountains. But this time, before awakening, one thing was certain. I had to go there.

The Sutra

"If you want to go to Shambhala, there are many dangerous places and demons will disrupt the way and hurt you on the road... Many people will try to be obstacles... If you read the sutra many times, through mental power, you will overcome them."

Shambhala Sutra

Tashilumbo Monastery is located in Tibet's central-western city of Shigatze. Here, wind blows through long winding corridors of packed stone, leaving cool vacuums of space between the flattening heat of late afternoon. This time of the day in central-western Tibet, one can feel feverish. Golden rays become razor knives slicing laterally across the Himalayan plateau. Their intensity sharpens as the late afternoon sun shifts.

This is the best time of the day to take refuge from the sun. Between the coolness of thick adobe walls, a monk enters a corridor. His robes are touched by wind. He tightens them against the cold. The corridor is dark. It leads into cool space brightened by dark wooden block prints stacked into walls. The wooden blocks are so closely packed into the walls that not even a rat can find its way through the maze created by them.

These wood blocks are used for printing sutras (Tibetan prayer books). Sutras contain more than prayers. They tell stories of the past and future. They can provide meditation instruction. If read carefully between the lines, they drop hints, like where to go next.

Sutras are printed by hand. This is not because the Tibetans do not have digitized offset printing systems, or that multinational software companies have not penetrated the Tibetan plateau—believe me, they are everywhere. When printing sutras, the monks recite prayer blessings and mantra. This goes beyond the functions of a digitized offset printing system. There are just some things with which advanced technology still cannot yet connect.

Two young novice monks are dusting and re-ordering the block prints. This is a kind of library inventory. There is no Internet depository of information here. Only old boxes made of wood and yak skin. But they are very reliable and can weather the hot summers and cold winters. Tucked inside each box is a sutra.

One black yak skin box is removed from a shelf and placed on a table very carefully. An old sutra text — the only one left of its kind — is wrapped and placed back into the box with tender care only given to a baby. There is no other sutra like this one left in the world. There are no copies, only this original. It is called "Shambhala Sutra".

The Sixth Panchen Lama, Losang Palden Yeshe (1737-1780), wrote the *Shambhala Sutra*. Tashilumbo Monastery has always been the seat of the Panchen Lamas. So their main palace is here. The last precious copy of the ancient *Shambhala Sutra* is kept in the palace. Access to it is limited.

The sutra was written on at least three different levels.

On the first level, it can be understood as a guidebook leading one on a journey to find the mystical kingdom of Shambhala. This kingdom is sometimes referred to in western literature as "Shangri-La". So on a first read, it appears that *Shambhala Sutra* serves as a roadmap, a kind of Tibetan odyssey.

Shambhala Sutra describes places such as "Poison Lake", "Demon Lake" and "one hundred mountains that emit light after dark" — a natural Himalayas aurora borealis phenomenon. All these places exist in Ngari, Tibet's most western, remote and inaccessible prefecture. By following *Shambhala Sutra* as a guidebook, sure enough one can arrive at these places. I found them by making this journey; they all exist. But the question remains — can the sutra lead you to Shambhala?

On a second level, maybe the sutra is not meant to be a literal travel guide at all. Another interpretation is: it could be a meditation roadmap leading each individual on a journey within himself. At this level, the understanding of *Shambhala Sutra* becomes more complicated. It teaches each of us how to harness negative energy and convert it into positive. But can we do it?

There is a third-level understanding. *Shambhala Sutra* serves as an oracle of events yet to come, a kind of Nostradamus prediction. Many might prefer

to just dismiss this part. However, maybe we have already arrived upon certain events without realizing it.

The sutra prophesizes the Kali Age, or the era of destruction. It tells of one nation, specifically in the west that adheres to a religious and political ideology of intolerance. It tries to unite the world into a single empire, seeking to impose its values and beliefs on other nations and peoples. Meanwhile, people in its own cities kill one another for greed. Control of resources to support wasteful luxury at the expense of other peoples is an underlying premise of the empire's expansion. Environmental desecration becomes part of the process.

Reaction becomes violent as weaker peoples, whose voices are not heard, use guerilla tactics to fight back. They adopt even unthinkable methods to counter the massive force of religious values and political ideologies being globally imposed upon them. They return to caves and tunnel networks in the

mountains, resorting to extreme measures because all other legitimate options have run out. The sutra specifically foresees the rise of 'terrorist actions'. Some scholarly interpretations indicate the spark unleashing the Kali Age will occur in Central Asia, what is today's Afghanistan.

Negative actions breed negative reactions, which in turn stimulate an irreversible cycle of war and suffering. The Kali Age of war, terror and disease is driven by an underlying cycle of human ignorance and short-term greed perpetuated through a very advanced economic system based on belief in the overwhelming driving force of materialistic motivation.

The cycle only ends when a new world order arrives. This requires a complete shattering of assumptions underlying the earlier world order. The sutra envisions

suppressing negative forces with a positive universal intention to herald a future era of peace, environmental balance and human dignity yet to come. This future is Shambhala.

Shambhala Sutra tells of a road to 'a place beyond a place.' This place seems unreachable, but it can be attained. The sutra suggests how to attain it. Within the Shambhala Sutra, prophecies written in the past become relevant to the future. So because Shambhala Sutra is a kind of oracle, it is invaluable.

Shambhala Sutra is not available on the Internet, so do not bother trying to find it there. There is only one hard copy left. It is kept in the sutra library in Tashilumbo Monastery. Here, it is very safe.

A monk caringly wraps the ancient sutra in an orange cloth and tucks it back into an old oiled black yak skin box, which is then carefully placed on a wooden table soaked in blue light from yak butter candles flickering for a moment from movement of his robes as he passes into the next chamber.

Two novices follow the monk. They are very careful in learning and studying his every action. Together, they leave, finding a place down the corridor to rest for a moment and sip Tibetan tea. But when they return, they are shocked. The unforeseen has occurred. The black box is missing.

The Directions

"Then paint the woman demon again
and offer meat of many animals. She will appear.
Ask her to show the way."

Shambhala Sutra

Things start later in Lhasa. Clocks are fixed to Beijing time, but local people continue to follow the sun. It was already 9:30 a.m. but the narrow whitewashed adobe alleyways of Lhasa's old city were just beginning to awake.

For many Tibetans, morning begins by encircling Jokhang Temple or Potala Palace. They turn handheld prayer wheels with a feeling of grace. They remember what they have awoken for.

At 3,600 meters above sea level, breathing becomes acute, a bit more difficult. Having just arrived in Lhasa, everything felt as if it had begun in slow motion. Taking one's time becomes important, which is actually essential. This means using the space around you to think before doing.

I thought about this for a moment, taking a breath. It was the first time I did that. Having arrived the night before, I still felt wheezy from the altitude. Stopping before a stall selling Tibetan flat bread for breakfast, I asked, "How much is one piece?"

"Five 'jiao' (fifty cents)," the shop lady smiled. As I pulled five Chinese ten cents bills from my pocket, three children rushed up and tugged at my sleeves, hands held out, begging. I handed the fifty cents to the stall lady. Smiling, she leaned over and gave each begging child one ten-cent bill. "Now go, leave the foreigner alone," she laughed, as the kids ran off giggling.

I was stunned. She sold me Tibetan bread for fifty cents, but gave most of it away to begging children. With only twenty cents in her hand, she was technically losing money on the bread sale. Such a simple act of selfless giving does not happen frequently. I thought, what if such a situation were to occur in Beijing, Shanghai, or Guangzhou, where people would think of every possible way to cheat fifty cents from a foreigner? They would probably fight among themselves for not giving a single cent away, much less giving it to begging children at a sales loss. Coming from Beijing and Hong Kong, where I lived and worked as a

lawyer, this sudden look into Tibetan thought juxtaposed and shook all of my thinking about China.

Like every visitor who has just arrived in Lhasa, I took a tour of the Potala Palace, then the Norbulinka Summer Palace. Afterwards, I wandered through the Barkor Market, where pilgrims circumambulated Jokhang Temple, probably Tibet's most sacred site. Around Barkor Market, tourists looked for antique gifts to bring back home. By accident, I wandered into a tiny shop.

A Kham lady beckoned me in. Her name was La Zha. "We have *thankas*, Buddhas, everything. What would you like?" she blurted enthusiastically.

"Anything that is old... Do you have any antiques?"

"Everything is antique," she assured me. "Don't you know, antique is a style."

I began to feel suspicious. "No, I am looking for real antiques, you know, very old things."

"Old?"

"Yes, I am looking for very old things."

"Very old?" she looked perplexed, sitting down on a large Tibetan rug in the back of her shop. "If it is not old enough, we can make it look older." Then pensively, she waved me to sit down beside her. "How old is 'old'?"

"I mean a real antique, not something made today, or even yesterday."

She laughed. "There are very few really old things around these days," she shrugged.

"But I have real things, of course, all real. But you say you want one, which is 'real' and really old too? That may be difficult to find, but not so difficult, because I have a friend who had received something from another friend, and has asked me if I could keep it in my shop and sell it to anyone who wanted to buy it. But most people do not want to buy it."

"Why?"

"Because they do not know what it really is."

"What is it?" I asked, my curiosity growing.

"I don't know. But if you would like to look at it, I can show it to you."

She then dusted off a shelf, moving back several stone Buddha statues. From behind, she lifted a heavy elongated box made of wood that was tightly wrapped with blackened yak skin, secured by iron brooches nailed to the box. Clearly, it had been hidden behind the new stone Buddha, which was made to look old.

"What's this?"

"It is very old."

"I can see that. But what is it?"

"It is from a friend's friend who…"

"I know, you told me. But where is it from? Exactly, what is it?"

"It is from Shigatze."

"Where is it from?"

"Shigatze," she whispered. "It comes from Tashilumbo Monastery."

"Tashi — what? Where is this place?"

"It is another city about one day's drive from Lhasa. Shigatze is the sacred city of His Holiness, the Panchen Lama. The monastery of the Panchen Lama is called Tashilumbo. It is also known as the Palace of Infinite Light."

"Palace of…"

"…Infinite Light."

"Then this is from the Panchen Lama's palace, right? That's what you are telling me?"

"Yes," she said cautiously.

"How did you get it?"

"A friend's friend…"

"Ok, I know. And he gave it to you to sell, right?"

"This is really old."

"Yes, I can see, it is really old."

"It is the best thing in my shop. If you want, it can be yours."

"How much is it?"

"How much are you willing to pay?"

I looked at the box. "It's not what I am willing to pay," I tried to reason with the shop lady. "It is whether I want this or not. I still don't know what this is."

She leaned over and opened the box. The fingers of her two hands were covered in turquoise and silver jewelry. Between the elegance of faded turquoise, she opened the old box, releasing fragrant yak oil smells.

Amidst the fragrance was an orange cloth bound tightly around a stack of fragile, brown, faded papers. "What are these?" I asked, dumbfounded.

"My friend said his friend told him this is the *Shambhala Sutra*."

"Sham ... what?"

"*Shambhala Sutra*. How much are you willing to pay?"

We haggled. It took a while. Somehow, she convinced me that I must have the *Shambhala Sutra*. It was a real antique, and this I could tell from the smells in the box. In turn, I tried to convince her that I was a poor trekker and could not afford to pay the price she asked. She did not believe me.

"Purchasing something is not a question of buying or selling," a voice whispered behind me. I turned around, surprised to see a young girl enter the shop. "The turquoise in my ring fell out," she called over to La Zha. "Can you help me fix it?" She seemed to know La Zha quite well. Then looking at me sitting on the rug holding the sutra, she leaned over and added as half an afterthought waiting irresistibly to be spoken, "It is not a question of economics or price parity against affordable income. Rather, it is a question of whether something belongs to you or not, whether it will become yours, and where you will go with it, or where it will take you."

"Who are you?" I asked.

"I run the teahouse next door, upstairs in the old yellow stone building over there," she pointed upwards in a direction lazily with a long finger protruding

from a ring with a piece of turquoise missing. "La Zha, can you please arrange somebody to fix this," she implored the antique dealer, half jokingly pleading for help.

She then sat down on the rug next to me, fingering the edge of the black sutra box with the same outstretched finger. "If something does not belong to you, then regardless of the rational market value, do not take it. If something comes to you without asking, then it is yours without question. If it is taken without asking, then it will not belong to you, but by coincidence it can take you to where you want to go, instead of letting you follow the wrong directions from which disentanglement may be difficult. This is not a factor of supply and demand but the natural possessing and disposing of energy. Such coincidence may, in your mind, sound irrational. But in Tibetan Buddhism, we believe there is no such thing as coincidence."

"Who are you, really? An economist working for some NGO here?"

"Actually," she sighed, sitting cross-legged and placing elbows on both knees, the jeans of which were torn into shreds as if a cat had been clawing her legs. "I am just a nomad. I did not even graduate from high school. I never had the patience to study."

"You didn't graduate from high school? Then where did you pick up all this economic talk? You sound like someone from Brookings or a talking head on CNN."

"That must be because of my nomadic background. We like to move from one place to another. I bet they didn't tell you that on *Discovery Channel* or *National Geographic* either. You see, we nomads get disillusioned from changes in weather. We have an innate understanding of how to avoid storms."

I had had enough and stood up. Paying for the sutra box, I heard the clinging of her ring as she dropped it on the counter. "La Zha, can you fix this for me?" her voice called behind me. Leaving La Zha's shop without turning back, I continued to wander through Barkor Market looking for antiques. She followed.

"Ok," I asked. "What's your name?"

"Renzhen Deki."

"Ren-zhen – De- what?"

"Renzhen Deki. 'Renzhen' means 'precious jewel'. 'Deki' means 'reaching new heights'. In Buddhism, we have many precious jewels. If you carry one with you and wish upon it, maybe it can take you to new heights."

We walked between the stands. "By the way," she added almost as an afterthought. "That sutra you carry under your arm, the one you just bought, it is real. I mean it's something really old."

"How old is it?"

"I don't know. Did La Zha tell you where it came from?"

"She said it was from the Panchen Lama's monastery, I think she said Tashilumbo. She claims it is the *Shambhala Sutra*. I have no way of knowing what it really is."

"Do you want to know?"

"Of course, but how does one find out?"

"In Jokhang Temple, there is a famous monk named Nyima Tsering. He will know. If you want, I can take you to see him."

"Ok."

As she led me toward the entrance of Jokhang Temple, with the pilgrims prostrating, sunlight crossed her dark skin. She wore an Indian batik shirt, torn in the back. Thick silver and turquoise jewelry dangled everywhere on her body. One strand of hair crossing her face was dyed yellow. Another strand was braided with tiny knots in traditional Tibetan style favored by nomads. Tied at the tip of her braids was a tiny bone carving. I would have barely noticed it, except it caught the afternoon sunlight. It was a carving of an outstretched hand with one eye on its palm.

Suddenly, I felt somebody grab my wrist. I was startled, confused. A man in yellow shirt pressed his forehead against my wrist. I froze, unsure as to what to do. For a moment, I thought he might try to take something from me, maybe a ploy to pick my pocket. I reached for my pocket, but my wallet was there. I was completely wrong. Instead, he continued pressing his head against my wrist even harder. I did not know what to do or why he was doing this. Looking around, I quickly turned to Renzhen Deki. "Why is he doing this?"

"He is doing this because you are holding the sutra."

As we walked toward the entrance of Jokhang Temple, she recited something in a bare whisper while shifting beads between long thin fingers.

I noticed a string of ivory Buddhist prayer beads around her tiny wrist. The pure white contrasted sharply against her smooth skin, shining almost gold in Lhasa's afternoon sun. I asked about the white beads.

Renzhen Deki explained, "They were given by a wandering traveler who could see the future because he was haunted by the past. He gave me these ivory prayer beads as a gift because white is the color of purity. Before leaving, he asked me to remain pure in a world that is already polluted with corruption and greed. The last thing he did was leaving me instructions to recite the mantra of White Tara."

"White who --?"

"White Tara is a Bodhisattva with eyes on her hands, feet and forehead. She can see all sufferings and is dedicated to helping people on their way. The day this wanderer left, I began reciting her mantra. I have never stopped reciting it."

I listened to the story but could not quite follow. Actually, it did not make any sense. "What's a Bodhisattva?" I asked.

"Those who choose to stay back."

"Choose? They have a choice?"

"We always have a choice."

"Then what do these Bodhisattvas do?"

"They lead people to the right direction."

The Monk

"Hermit monks will welcome and carry you
to Shambhala...But if you have not reached this
level of meditation then it won't happen and
you must continue on your own journey."

Shambhala Sutra

At the door of Jokhang Temple, Renzhen Deki left. I was not sure where she went. Maybe back into the crowd. I was about to look but I could not see into the crowd. Too many people were prostrating before the temple's great door. Others sat under the bright red columns on stone slabs smoothed from prostration, mixing seeds or glass crystals into silver rings.

I was trying to figure out what they were doing. Then a monk appeared from within to ask if he could help. He sensed my confusion. I began explaining how I had been led by this girl to Jokhang Temple to look for a famous monk.

The monk just pointed to the black box under my arm. "That sutra you carry, where did you get it?"

"I bought this from an antique store at Barkor Market. The seller claimed it is the *Shambhala Sutra*. Who knows? But I want to find out. So I came here to ask a monk named Nyima Tsering."

"I am Nyima Tsering." Swoosh, saffron robe flung over a shoulder, he led me in between the vast yak oiled doors of Jokhang Temple. Within, we sat down on woven yak fur meditation mats in the dim flickering light of yak butter candles. He opened the yak skin black box and removed the sutra that was wrapped tightly in orange cloth. I suddenly became aware that every aspect of life in Tibet is one way or another connected to yaks.

Then gently touching the sutra to the top of his head with respect, Nyima Tsering unfolded the orange cloth and began fingering worn browned pages of sutra text. "It is true," he exclaimed. "This is *Shambhala Sutra*. It was written by His Holiness, the Sixth Panchen Lama many years ago."

"But what is *Shambhala Sutra*?"

"It is a guidebook to Shambhala. If you want to search for it, the sutra can take you there. The question is whether you are willing to follow it or not."

I was becoming curious. "Can you explain, by following this sutra, how I can really reach Shambhala?"

"If you really want to follow it, I suggest that you first find a Rimpoche — 'Living Buddha'. Such a very learned Tibetan spiritual leader will know. Only with his guidance can it be used properly to find the correct path to Shambhala."

"Sorry, but can you explain to me what is Shambhala?"

"Shambhala is a pure ideal realm of our consciousness," he whispered with half a sigh and a smile. "It is a return to a world of peace and happiness. This is what we really mean by Shambhala."

"You mean it is not some place, like Shangri-La?"

"It is really not as complicated as we lead ourselves to believe," he explained. "Think for a moment. All humanity and sentient forms of life seek only two things — first their survival, then their happiness. Have you ever asked how we lose these — first our happiness, then our ability to survive? Maybe we are regressing, about to make ourselves extinct."

I thought about global warming, wars in the Middle East and seemingly everywhere else at the same time. It seemed as if the whole world is at war with itself. "Yes, maybe this is happening to us," I said out loud.

"Cycles of environment, the order of our universe, brings about results naturally. When we break this order, the results are unnatural." Nyima Tsering explained. "Our natural world possesses an intrinsic warning system. We are just ignoring it. We are forgetting our natural self."

"Why? We have the resources to do something about it, don't we?"

"We humans think we are more intelligent because we have physical intelligence, but maybe this logical intelligence has actually cost us our spiritual intelligence, our intuition. So warnings go unheeded. In the end, humanity driven by shortsighted interests and greed ignores its instincts and adopts methods, bringing negative results. This gives rise to the disasters we face today."

"So we are ignoring the warnings, putting the inevitable on the backburner,

is that what you mean?"

Nyima Tsering's eyes widened. "Often, we see a disaster on the news and blame it on events, or on somebody else. It was not our fault, it must be their fault, we say. Some other people, organization or even demonic force did this to us. Actually, we must blame each of these events on ourselves."

"But why blame ourselves if somebody else did it?"

"In Buddhism we have a concept of causational effect. We explain each effect as being precipitated by a cause. Ultimately, one way or another, we are that cause."

"Ok," I tried to change the subject. "If this sutra is supposed to be a guidebook to Shambhala, then how am I going to get there?"

"*Shambhala Sutra* is a guidebook that tells you how to get there. It is also a kind of oracle. It foretells the Kali Yulga, or 'Age of Destruction', and an epic

war already upon us."

"You mean like the end of the world? Like what they talk about in the Bible — Noah and the floods in the Old Testament and the Last Judgment in the New Testament?"

"No. When we talk about the 'Age of Destruction,' it is a completely different concept from these. We do not mean some spirit or demon coming to destroy the world. No. Nor do we divide our world into periods of war and peace with clear distinction between the two. There is no external god who determines this, no greater judge. Actually, we serve as our own judge. In fact, this 'Age of Destruction' is determined by our own karma. Neither is it something fixed in a book, locked into a calendar. If our negative karma can be turned into positive karma, then the 'Age of Destruction' can be delayed indefinitely. The wheel will have turned another cycle. Then we can bring about an age of peace in our own lifetime. This will be the era of Shambhala. The question comes down to our own collective attitude."

"So the 'Age of Destruction' is not some black judgment day?"

"No. Now it is already part of our own 21st Century reality. We have hoped that this era would be enriched with high technology, better medical care, and rational minds sitting down at the United Nations stopping wars before they start. But instead, we are witnessing many unthinkable events, such as terrorism, wars, natural disasters, and diseases such as SARS, the avian flu, and AIDS. Why do we face such catastrophes, both man-made and natural? This is because we now have a collective problem with our karma."

"So what do we do about these collective karma problems?"

"We should seek out what we all already have within," he explained frankly. "Actually, each person begins life with a pure heart. But external factors, events and many impurities enter and pollute each person's consciousness. Many horrible events unfold as a result. This is not because some other person or force has done this to us. It is because we have done it to ourselves. It is our own actions precipitating these events."

I was quite confused by what he was saying. On one hand, he talked about taking a trip using the sutra as a guidebook. On the other hand, he talked about the trip being within. I was not sure whether he expected me to come or go. The simple purchase of an antique sutra box was now creating a confusing mess out of what I thought might be a nice holiday in Tibet off the beaten track. I asked him to explain what trip he expected me to take with this sutra guidebook and how much further it would lead.

"Actually, if you embark on this journey, to follow the *Shambhala Sutra*, you will find it is not just a guidebook to a place, but a guidebook to within. Our bodies are *mandalas*, mere microcosms of the universe. When you see the monks and nuns sitting on the stone floor of Jokhang Temple mixing seeds and crystals in different tiered rings, they are making *mandalas*."

"What do they do after they make one of these?"

"They give it as an offering to the universe of which we are just a tiny but intrinsically inseparable part. After making such an offering with their minds and positive intentions, they take apart the *mandalas* by dismantling the rings and dispersing sand or crystals. Then they make it again. If you journey to Shambhala, the trip will be like entering a *mandala*. In the end, you will just be entering your own self. Like the *mandala*, you can take it apart and start again."

The Buddha

"If you cannot find it, meditate."

Shambhala Sutra

I climbed the yak butter soaked stairwell in the yellow stone building to Renzhen Deki's teahouse. I found her sitting on a couch, ignoring the customers and reading a clothbound book. Actually it was a notebook. I was to learn later that she had written all the notes in the book herself. In the teahouse, she always kept it on the table before her.

Looking up from the book, at first saying nothing, she then smiled. "Table for one?" I sat down on the couch in front. She leaned over, "What did teacher Nyima Tsering say?"

"It is really the *Shambhala Sutra*. But to use it as a guidebook to Shambhala, he said, I will need to seek the teachings of a high-ranking lama, what you Tibetans call a Rimpoche or 'Living Buddha'. Do you know where I can find such a master?"

She thought about the question for a while but did not answer. After drinking several cups of tea, I felt this was not going anywhere so I offered to pay the bill. She tore up the bill with her sharp fingernails and just told me to wait outside Jokhang Temple's front door on Saturday afternoon. That was her day off.

I waited on Saturday. She appeared from the crowd, wrapped in a nomad blanket, wearing designer sunglasses, both arms covered with even more silver and turquoise bracelets. Her ivory prayer beads were wrapped tightly around her left wrist.

We took a taxi to a place called Chakpori Hill. Here, she explained, was where Songtsen Gampo, the first king to unify Tibet under Buddhism, often came to meditate. Sometimes, during festival holidays, Renzhen Deki came here as well to turn prayer wheels.

Beside the hill is a cliff. It is carved with literally hundreds of carvings of Buddha, Bodhisattvas and Guardians. Before the cliff, Tibetans prostrate

in homage. She explained how they clasp their hands above their head for Buddha, then to their chest for the Teachers or Gurus, then to their waist for the Bodhisattvas. Lastly, they lay outstretched flat upon the earth for the Guardians who protect. They do this every day. Renzhen Deki explained, on important festivals, she would often just leave her teahouse, regardless of how many customers might be there, and prostrate this way all along the pilgrimage route of Barkor, circumambulating Jokhang Temple.

"It is an expression of total devotion to the energy these forces represent. These are interactive powers of the universe. They can lead us on our way and protect us," Renzhen Deki explained. "When I am prostrating in the street, reciting my mantra, it feels good. Even when crowds step on my back, and legs, or kick my head, I feel no anger, only compassion. We are equal before all. In moments like this, I recite my mantra to myself, to deepen the meaning in my mind. It is a feeling of complete oneness with the universe."

Still not understanding, I pointed to different carvings on the huge rocks and asked which Bodhisattva was the one she had talked about the other day. Ignoring my question, she led me along a path of spinning prayer wheels. She shrugged and as an afterthought, "No need for me to tell you. But it cannot hurt for you to ask."

"Why?"

"When the time is right, you will already know it yourself."

The prayer wheels led up a narrow path beside the hill, a sharp stone surface jutting upwards toward the blue sky above, dotted by fragile clouds that seemed ready to crack with the whisper of her breath. Touching the wheels gently, each turning ever so slowly, she said nothing, just walked along the path. The sky did not crack, and the blue remained impenetrable.

I followed her under the prayer flags to a place where His Eminence, Beru Khyentse Rimpoche — one of Tibet's powerful Living Buddhas — sat half smiling

among a shade of prayer flags fluttering in wind. He observed prayer flags with a presence that did not need extra attention. Everything in his mind had an appropriate place. It was already understood. So when people, confused by the frustrations of life, sought out his advice, he could clearly identify the location of each frustration. He was able to help people this way, by rearranging the energy.

A crowd of Tibetan pilgrims were lining up before him, bowing and asking for his blessings. One after another, they shifted closer in sequential order, seeking his touch. He placed his hand on the head of each. One by one, vanishing from where they had been kneeling, each returned to where they had come from. As almost an afterthought remembered but not quite forgotten, Beru Khyentse Rimpoche looked at me approaching. Precipitating my question, he asked nothing.

Renzhen Deki prostrated three times, knelt down and bent her head downwards toward the ground, edging closer. Beru Khyentse Rimpoche touched the top of her head with his wide palm flat open.

I began to ask ecstatically about *Shambhala Sutra*. He nodded his shaven round head, resting at such ease upon his large rounded body. Possessing the appearance of a great Buddha statue smiling at the entrance to a temple, enormous but serene, he whispered, "This is not appropriate time. First hang up the prayer flags."

I was taken aback. Holding *Shambhala Sutra* in my hand, I wanted answers. Instead, I did not even get questions, but an order to hang up prayer flags. I turned to Renzhen Deki. She just smiled, indicating I should follow one of his monks already standing on the sharp precipice above trying to throw a string of prayer flags over all the other strings and tie it to a rock. So somebody was needed to catch the string and tie it. I fumbled up the rocks and reached out for the string. Sunlight caught my eye and a foot slipped.

"Before you try to follow the road to Shambhala, both feet must be firm on the ground," Beru Khyentse Rimpoche smiled.

I got my grip with both hands grasping the rocks. They turned to dust and I slipped again before regaining balance. I now began to listen to what he was saying. Things became easier. I tied the prayer flags. The string hung loose before it tightened. A wind had caught the flags like kites. They fluttered following wind.

"Remember," Beru Khyentse Rimpoche nodded toward the flags crackling in the breeze. "The size of a fire is not determined by how heavy the log placed upon it is. Rather, the force of fire is determined by the direction of wind. If you can control the direction of the wind, the force of fire will be yours to manipulate. If you do not understand how wind changes its course, the movement of energy, you may be burned. Or the fire will self extinguish before it is lit."

He then pointed to the sharp rock rising like knife stuck into the earth. "This rock was where Tibet's first Dharma king Songtsen Gampo often came to meditate," Beru Khyentse Rimpoche explained. "His meditation caves are here in the rock. He was a very wise king who unified Tibet under Buddhism and made marriage alliances with Nepal and China. This way he avoided conflicts and made peace with all sides around him."

"He must have been a wise diplomat," I commented. "It seemed he took the best of both cultures and combined them, without excluding either."

"If you look at images of Songtsen Gampo flanked by his two wives, the Chinese princess holds an offering cup of wine in her hand, while the Nepalese princess holds the Dharma wheel in hers," Beru Khyentse Rimpoche pointed out. "One alliance was political, the other spiritual. Both were Bodhisattvas. We say one was the manifestation of Green Tara, the other White Tara. Remember, politics and spirituality cannot be separable. The two Taras are in fact one."

"How did he keep his two wives from having conflict?" I asked incredulously.

"The king kept them in separate palaces of course," Beru Khyentse Rimpoche smiled.

I then decided to follow and do as Renzhen Deki did, prostrating three times and kneeling down before handing Beru Khyentse Rimpoche the *Shambhala Sutra*. I asked whether Shambhala was really 'Shangri-La,' that place depicted in the movie by the Hollywood director John Capra. The movie was based on a book *Lost Horizon* written by an Englishman named James Hilton.

Beru Khyentse Rimpoche explained that 'Shangri-La' is really 'Shambhala,' spelled incorrectly by a western author who did not know what he was writing about. Neither author nor director ever visited Tibet or even Asia for that matter. The result is today, most people think of Shangri-La as a luxury hotel chain.

"Shambhala is a pure land," he explained clearly. "Our land is pure, but some people are not pure. While there are pure people and holy people, there are also 'negative' people who do not respect the ways of 'karma'. They use negative energy, which creates reciprocal negative energy. The result is global wars, incurable diseases, environmental destruction, ultimate disaster."

"Cumulated negative energy and action brings about 'Kali Yulga' or the 'Kali Age of Destruction,' he explained. According to prophecies, these events occur approximately 2,300 years after the first Buddha Sakyamuni's death, which means we are now in the Kali Age."

Beru Khyentse Rimpoche continued, explaining, "The Kali Age witnesses an endless cycle of war, environmental desecration, pestilence, and disease. Many diseases we have never heard of arise. Diseases like AIDS and SARS, which cannot be cured. More diseases will come. The cause is brought about by our own negative actions."

"When negative intention is the cause, negative events result," Beru Khyentse Rimpoche quietly observed. How can positive change follow, with funding of government and commercial priorities being negatively intended? All effects derive from cause. All cause derives from intention. If your intention is negative or positive, the results following will be either negative or positive.

This will set off a chain of karmic events. Sometimes, it is hard to undo what has been done. So what we do next becomes all the more important."

"Before, even the food we ate was pure, with nutrients from earth's minerals and the sun's energy," explained Beru Khyentse Rimpoche. "Now, it is processed with chemicals and few vitamins. We can eat a lot today, but receive very little in required nutrients. This is caused by our own actions and impurities, which destroy the environment and, in turn, our way of living."

"So if I follow this sutra like a roadmap, will I be able to find Shambhala?"

"Of course you can find it. But only if your intention is right will you be able to find it. By the way," he asked. "You are not a trekker?"

"No."

"What is your real profession?"

"I am a lawyer."

"Oh. Do you know as a Living Buddha, what is my profession?"

"No?"

"I am a Dharma lawyer."

"Then can you tell me which way I should go? North or south?"

"Try going west. Go to Mount Kailash."

"When I get there, will I have reached Shambhala?"

"Of course not," he frowned, then smiled.

"Then what should I do when I get to Mount Kailash?"

"Meditate."

"Meditate? How do you do that?"

He folded his legs underneath his body. They seemed to disappear. He then folded both hands and began breathing. "Like this," he advised. "When you breathe in, absorb all the positive energy. Believe me, there is a lot of it around, you just cannot see it. You never paid attention to its existence. When you breathe out, reject the negative. Actually, you do not need it. Think about absolutely nothing at all. It is the elimination of duality."

"Duality?"

"Actually, there are no opposites. So eliminate this from your mind as a concept. You will then become one with yourself because you will accept non-duality."

"What does that mean?"

"That means there will be no attachment to the things you thought were important holding on to, because you will realize they were never important. It is only extra luggage you are trying to check in when all you really need is a small carry-on. If you can achieve this way of thinking, then there will be nothing to think about."

"But how can you think about nothing when there are so many things to think about?

"You think too much about things around you, which in reality are unimportant." He smiled with half a chuckle that never became a laugh.

"But we have to live in reality," I insisted, "don't we?"

Beru Khyentse Rimpoche smiled. "Just always remember one thing about reality: it does not exist."

The Oracle

"In fact every day there is killing among the people living in city buildings with many doors. Their way is to commit negative action, disease arises... because they want to make the whole world the same as theirs."

Shambhala Sutra

I went back to Jokhang Temple, entering the thick yak oil and incense soaked doors before which hundreds of Tibetan pilgrims prostrate daily. Inside sitting on a raised dais together with other monks, I found Nyima Tsering. Upon seeing me, he stood up, anticipating my question before it could be asked. When I asked it, he led me into the monastery's main courtyard.

The courtyard is surrounded by ancient paintings, many depicting aspects from the life of the first Buddha Sakymuni. From here, the inner circumambulation routes lead clockwise around the original Jokhang complex, built by the Nepalese wife of Tibet's first king Songtsen Gampo. She had brought craftsmen to build the temple. Even today, oiled unpainted wooden pillars and beams within depict figures carved in Nepalese style.

The 'Jowo,' or main Buddha figure, lies within Jokhang's inner crypt. It was brought from the Tang Emperor's court and presented to Songtsen Gampo by his second wife, Princess Wencheng.

Tossing his saffron monk's robe over one shoulder with ease, Nyima Tsering led me to the left, along the path of prayer wheels. We followed Tibetan pilgrims turning wheels. We began turning them ourselves.

Starting from the first row of brass wheels, he showed me how to turn each one slowly with deliberation. He explained that each wheel has the mantra of compassion written upon it and prayers rolled up within. Turning prayer wheels can be understood on multiple levels. Turning a wheel spins the mantra within. It is also the beginning of a cycle. People following the circumambulation route turn consecutive wheels, one after another. This means they travel a cyclical path. This is the route we follow, life after life.

That's why you will always find so many Tibetans at the temples in the morning and at dusk. Turning the wheels at this time especially expresses that

wherever we are today at night is where we begin tomorrow. That is the time when dawn arrives.

"Do you know," I asked. "The word 'revolution' in English means literally the complete 360 degree turning of a wheel."

Nyima Tsering's eyes lit when he heard this. I realized there was something he wanted to say but was waiting for the opportunity. As we came to the last row of prayer wheels, at the long corridor's end as it came full circle back to the inner temple's entrance, he showed me the mural of Shambhala. It was hidden behind a protective wire net painted on an old wall, unnoticed by most passing by.

I was surprised. The Shambhala mural did not depict pretty snow mountains, grasslands, with sheep, yaks and happy nomads as I had expected. Rather, the mural depicted a war. Troops were being sent to crush another army. I would not fully understand the meaning of this mural until I arrived at Tashilumbo Monastery — home of His Holiness the Panchen Lama — in Shigatze, almost a month later.

"Today our world is stricken with war," Nyima Tsering pointed to the detailed painting of troops jabbing each other with spears and swords. "Who started this war?" he asked out loud. "Some outside force or have we brought this deluge upon ourselves, through our own ill-thought actions?"

He then pointed to the black box I still carried under my arm. "Sure, look at what is written in *Shambhala Sutra*. It predicts everything like an oracle. It tells a story, how one day a leader, for his own prestige and driven by fanaticism of his own beliefs, will launch wars of destruction everywhere. He does not care about peace in the world or its people. He will even expend many lives of his own soldiers just to amass personal ambitions. He will try to conquer and unite nations which have no relationship with him without rational and calm consideration for the consequences. Ill-thought action running against the natural laws of Dharma will inevitably result in disaster for all involved." Pointing at the soldiers

annihilating themselves in the mural, he exclaimed, "Events backfire!"

"So that is what we see in the Shambhala mural," I asked, "an epic war of self-destruction? Is this what is happening today?"

He pointed out details. The mural depicting explosive projectiles and space ship like spiked wheels hovering over the troops. Clearly, whoever painted this mural centuries ago had some vision of what modern warfare would become; moreover, they understood where it would take us.

"Don't we have enough weapons like these?" Nyima Tsering asked. "Don't kid yourself. Every nation has them. Anyone can get them. But can we get rid of them? No. Now ask yourself one simple question. Can they blow up on their own? No. That is one thing I am certain of. These people understand the technology they are creating. Accidents of that kind just won't happen. They require somebody's intention to ignite those weapons. Someone has to decide

to do it. That is the starting point. The one who makes that decision is the problem."

"Can we turn the wheel back?" I asked.

"Remember, wheels cannot be turned backwards." He nodded toward the row of wheels we had just passed, now all spinning in tandem clockwise. "Our world state leaders should meditate and cure their own irrational mental illness because that is the real starting point of worldwide disasters," Nyima Tsering waved his hands in a gesture of simple frustration as he spoke. "I am sure if we had rational leaders who could calmly look at each developing situation in the world, they would not use these weapons and their technology for destructive purposes as it is happening today. It all begins with each person's greed and ignorance. If they can control their own greed and think intelligently in the context of broader rather than narrow interest, this mess would not be unfolding."

"Any hope for the peace process?"

"Look how these nations sign peace treaties," Nyima Tsering shook his

head in exasperation. "They are just cheating each other half the time. Even before the ink is dry, they are busy secretly making more weapons of mass destruction, planning to kill the same people they have just signed a treaty with. This is falsification."

"For them, it is business," I added. "They make big money manufacturing these weapons giving deals to their handpicked contractors. Taxpayers like us foot the bill. Then we have to bury our relatives when they come home in a box. They charge us death tax too."

Nyima Tsering seemed to be pondering details of the mural, where soldiers of Shambhala confront armies of greed and short-sight ignorance. "Some of our world's leaders have big mental problems," he sighed. "For their own aggrandizement, to be presidents, they will ruin and destroy many lives, including those of their own soldiers. Their thinking is actually quite stupid. They say: 'my nation is so great it will allow us to crush the others', but actually they only create the foundations for others to take revenge. This is common sense. Today someone from my side takes your life. Tomorrow someone from your side will take my life. This is an inevitable result of causational effect. The problem is not so complicated requiring theoretic studies and scenario running. What will happen is really quite obvious."

"But with all these think-tank organs and institutions overloaded with Stanford and Harvard professors, it seems amazing how simple logic has been thrown out the window," I commented.

"It is because intelligence is being misused," Nyima Tsering continued his thought, "So these people think they are really great. Oh, we can construct many weapons of mass destruction. Look, we have the capability and are so smart to develop all these weapons that can wipe out others so easily. Intelligence and resources should be used to cure disease, alleviate poverty and address our social ills. Then war will not arise. There will be no reason for it. So this endless creation of weaponry is the abuse of our human intelligence, not its rational application."

He led me up a stone stairwell between bright orange walls. "Too many people are blinded by short-term ignorance and greed. They cannot see in front, above or behind, like being trapped in a stairwell. If our own physical eyes cannot see what is happening, at least use our third eye, our intelligence, our thoughts, to see beyond the clouds. We'd better do something quickly. Otherwise, it will soon be too late."

We had reached the second floor. He led me down a long corridor behind a curtain, through a door and into his room. He reached over for a flask of yak butter tea, waving me to sit down. He opened the flask and poured a cup of tea.

"But they claim they have to do this to fight terrorism."

"Some nation's leaders think it can be destroyed crushing one nation after another. They believe through such process all the terrorists will eventually be eliminated. Think about it. Does this really make rational sense? If you look at what is really happening, it appears the more they try to crush the problem, the more it just multiplies."

"But they claim there is no other way," I wondered out loud. "The media never asks whether any other approach might work."

"The method they are adopting is wrong," Nyima Tsering said, pouring a cup of yak butter tea. "They believe force is everything in life and they can use power and money to crush others. This is impossible. Don't try to conquer others and crush them. Try to conquer yourself. If you really have such great culture and knowledge, then others will automatically follow you. But if you try to force them, then they will react against you and the result will be like an epidemic. Of course, the more you crush a people, the more they will come back to revenge."

"This way of thinking is not exclusive to Buddhism," I blurted out. "Just use common sense and you can see it."

"Please understand, we monks are not sitting here in Jokhang Temple every day telling people to become Buddhists. Rather, we are telling them to use rational intelligence for the common good. That way, the end result of all things is foreseeable. If one nation wants to use military force to tell others what to do, really, do you think they will happily follow? Maybe now, at this point in history, that particular nation has the power and force to crush them, but do you think by doing so, it will solve the real problem? This is only a temporary result. Problems will come back to haunt you, and they will grow worse."

"So from this perspective, the epic conflict depicted in the Shambhala mural can be understood on several levels?"

Nyima Tsering poured another cup of yak butter tea for both of us. "Remember, the leader who tries to conquer and rule other ethnic groups and peoples is not a hero but a criminal. The people who can stand up to crush their own greed, ignorance, and anger are the real heroes. Through their own examples, they can lead us on the right road. So these so-called world leaders should stop talking about what others should do to improve. They should improve themselves instead."

Vapor from melting yak butter rose. Its scent filled the room. Nyima Tsering continued with his thought unbroken as he re-filled both cups, "Both sides may be wrong, but this is not the starting point. If you keep attacking others' wrongs, then the problem will only escalate. The starting point is not with them, but yourself. If everyone begins with positive initiative — positive for you, for him, for them — then the overall result will be positive and we won't have this situation of international decay, war, disease and natural disaster. So my point is, calm down and think. Correct yourself, not others. Find out your own weakness and adjust within. Don't tell others what they should do. Go find the root of your own problem and fix it. Then you don't need to tell others how great your nation and way of life is, because if they see that what you are doing is right, they will naturally follow your example."

"Actually, those who are leading now have risen in a vacuum of leadership."

I held the hot teacup in both hands so as not to spill it, and took a sip. "Many are just puppets of defense and energy industries. So the source of funding decisions is in itself misguided."

"So that's why in Buddhism we place importance on the correct application of knowledge," Nyima Tsering stressed. "If you are a real leader, then better use your nation's knowledge, its resources and technology to lead other people toward happiness rather than blowing them into smithereens. Responsible leaders should begin by calming themselves, rationally subduing the three poisons within of greed, ignorance and anger. Only after subduing these should such person be qualified to be president of a nation or people. Just because you can blow up other people and take over a nation does not mean you are qualified to be president and actually lead anyone. Such views of heroism are completely distorted by Hollywood."

He poured another cup of yak butter tea. The smell warmed the coolness of Jokhang Temple's thick orange walls. "Think about it," Nyima Tsering said as I stared at my reflection in the smooth buttery surface filling the teacup. "All matter and events in our universe are connected. Nothing stands in its own isolation because one event will result in another. If you have disenfranchised a people, they will not sit back and take it, but will come back for revenge. It will take one form or another. If you kill somebody, his family will return to kill you. This is causational effect. Every action has a counter-reaction. If your action is positive, their reaction will be more positive. If your action is negative, it will breed negativity. If violent, it will be revenged."

He reached over to pour more tea. Almost as an afterthought, he added, "I hope all people, and particularly the citizens of certain particular countries, will begin to think rationally about what is happening. Calmly think it through. Our universe only has one world, that's it. It's our only home. Your life, my life, everyone's life is connected. Actually, there is only one life."

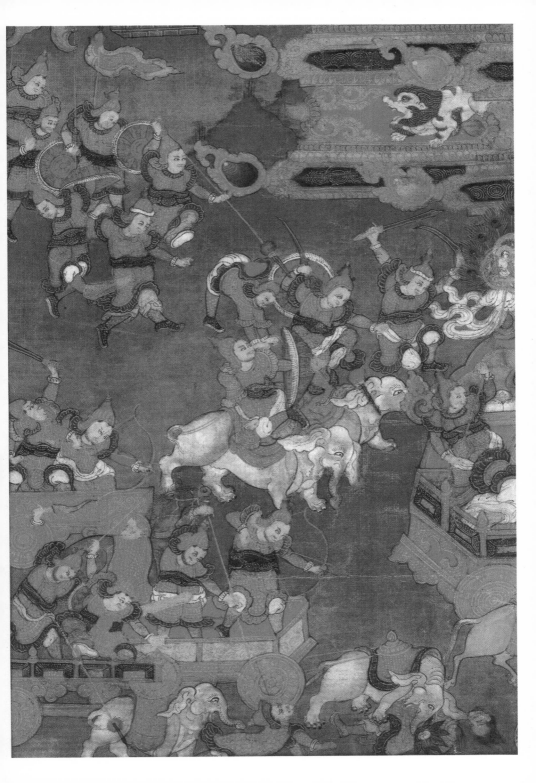

The Bodhisattva

"There is a Bodhisattva, a beautiful girl,
who wishes that all people
crossing from here will not be poor."

Shambhala Sutra

I came to understand Lhasa through Renzhen Deki's eyes. She often took me to the rooftop of Jokhang Temple, usually in the late afternoon when the sun stretches its fingertips into long shadows and the air begins to cool after a desert-like late summer afternoon. In the space when the day is not sure it will become night but is heading in that general direction, she would relax and talk about her childhood secrets, dreams of visiting New York and India, and one day seeing the ocean.

She had the greatest respect for her father, a doctor who left a stable job and salary with a hospital and traveled into remote regions of Qinghai to treat poor nomads. She talked about an uncle who was a monk, and a cousin — a 'Living Buddha' who had gone to India and came back. Renzhen Deki showed me how to read divinations with her prayer beads. She claimed to have been born with this talent, but refused to tell my fortune when I requested.

On weekends, she brought me to visit her aunt. She lived on the top floor of a Tibetan-style house tucked in a narrow alleyway which could be reached by following a slightly wider alley hidden near the entrance of Ramoche, a temple known to many Chinese as 'Little Jokhang.' The Chinese gave it this name because Ramoche housed the Buddha statue given to King Songtsen Gampo by his Nepalese wife, which was once kept in the main sanctum of Jokhang Temple before Songtsen Gampo's Chinese wife came along and switched it with the one she gave him. Things like that sometimes happened in those days. So the Tibetans built a second temple.

I used to wait outside this temple. Renzhen Deki would meet me there. She always appeared without warning from the crowd, sometimes wrapped in a nomad's blanket when the air seemed cool, sometimes sporting a Tibetan cowboy hat, when the sun was bright. Then each time, without saying anything, hurriedly,

she would lead me into the alley.

Her aunt's house was simple. The walls were orange, cracked and peeling in some places. Painted Tibetan motifs along the ceiling had long faded. Tibetan wood bed-chairs with rugs on them fit in an L-shape in the corner with a big wooden table between. The table was always covered with fruit and flat Tibetan bread on trays. Her aunt always served natural fresh yogurt with raw sugar on top. If you finished eating a bowl, she immediately refilled it.

In her late thirties, her aunt had three children. She possessed calm eyes, bright red cheeks, and long black hair kept in a single thick braid falling past her shoulders, straight down her back. Her aunt wore long Tibetan robes when going outside to blend with everyone in the street, unlike Renzhen Deki, who liked to wear torn shirts, flowing Indian batik skirts, and oversized silver and turquoise earrings conspicuously hidden behind designer sunglasses. The two women were externally a complete contrast but in actuality, they were the most intimate of souls. Renzhen Deki was emotional, but almost psychic in feeling all the moods and energy shifts around. Her aunt was steady and assuredly always knew what to do next. So in many ways, Renzhen Deki depended upon her aunt.

Later, after leaving Lhasa and returning to Beijing, visiting friends' comfortable big villas and meeting in sprawling modern offices with big glass windows looking out over infinite lights and traffic below, I often reflected back on her aunt's room, where somehow I felt more at home than any other place I had visited in my lifetime. I often thought that maybe Shambhala Palace is something like this, a simple room filled with afternoon sunlight and the magical quality of quietude. By sitting within such a space, it seemed enormous and luxurious, only because of the peace of mind it brought. After going back to the hustle of Beijing, my mind often returned to the warmth that filled those afternoons spent in her aunt's simple but honest home.

On those days, Renzhen Deki always sat on a Tibetan rug stretched on the wooden bed-chair before the window across from me. Afternoon light poured

through dusty glass panes in thin silk-like streams as if passing through stained glass in a cathedral. The light always seemed to touch the long hair glistening on the back of her shoulders.

During those weekend visits, time seemed to whittle away. Whole afternoons almost passed in seconds. We just sat there talking. After talking, we drank sweet Tibetan milk tea. I became aware of how time becomes distorted in our minds.

One day, Renzhen Deki unwrapped a white *hada* scarf and showed me a delicate gold plated image of a Bodhisattva. She was very happy. It had been blessed at Jokhang Temple the other day. Taking it with both hands, her aunt placed it on a shelf above us with an efficient sense of knowing what to do at the right time. "It is best placed here, in a high place, not on the table where you are both drinking tea."

I asked about the image. Renzhen Deki did not answer directly, but talked about another temple called Dromolakang. "It is the Tara Temple. When I first arrived in Lhasa, I went there. It gave me the warmest feeling, as if I had always belonged in that place. But since that visit, I have never gone back."

"So what does this have to do with the Bodhisattva your aunt just placed on the shelf there?"

"My Bodhisattva is White Tara."

I was curious and asked her to take me to Dromolakang. We waited until the following Saturday. Leaving Lhasa, we drove down the long road that eventually leads to the airport, then on to Shigatze. The Lhasa River flows into the Brahmaputra River, which flows alongside. It runs from the snows of Mount Kailash in western Tibet, east toward Lhasa, sharply turning southwest, and toward India and Bangladesh. Leaf tips of green trees lining the route were already turning gold as we drove down the long road. They had been penetrated by the earliest autumn wind. It whispered in a cool voice from a crystal blue sky that expectations were correct. Summer had now passed.

Dromolakang was along the roadside. I was not quite sure where. I might never have noticed and would have driven past it if Renzhen Deki had not pointed out the place. After stopping, it became clear that small brass prayer wheels line both sides of the entrance. Turning them, we stepped through the doorway.

In the central courtyard of Dromolakang sat a monkey, gray in color, with a square face and large hands, which were no different from any human being's, except they were smaller. The monkey squatted in the center of Dromolakang's courtyard. At night, he slept in the tree.

"Having lived many lives, he has traveled many roads. Otherwise he would not be living in this temple courtyard. It simply would not be allowed to happen." Renzhen Deki commented, tossing him a bag of peanuts, which I now realized had been brought along for the occasion. She then explained how a monkey can show the road you needed to travel on when you cannot

 *Going*

find the road, or when you have lost sight of all directions.

"It is in this point of confusion between compass points that one can come to understand the supreme knowledge of monkeys," Renzhen Deki added. "All monkeys are, one way or another, descendents of the Indian monkey king Hanumen. Legend says he could journey to all places and return from all directions at once in the blink of an eye. The Han Chinese adopted Hanumen into their legends of the mythical Monkey King, Sun Wukong. They tell the story of Sun Wukong being able to jump higher than anybody else, and his ability to change his size and shape. But he could never jump out of Buddha's palm."

"Why not?"

"Buddha's fingers were higher than mountains and his palm wider than the desert. The Monkey King felt overpowered, realizing the enormity of our universe, which is actually very tiny when you begin to think about it. Try and imagine all the other universes ours must be tucked within. We are really insignificant, maybe only a speck in Buddha's hand. The Monkey King was only fighting to overcome crevices between Buddha's fingers, but he thought they were mountains. So for all the Monkey King's magical powers, he still was frustrated by the effort of overcoming his own universe, because he had not yet discovered how to break the limitations of time and space through the unlimited power of emptiness."

"So what's the point of all these monkey stories," I was seeing all this cynically again.

"These stories send a message," she smiled tossing back strands of long black hair from her forehead with that sense of knowing something before you do, with the hinted pride of not wanting to reveal it all at once, but even keeping that pride a secret, or at least trying. "You can shatter perceptions and limitations of time and space by coming to terms with the oneness of all spherical emplacements. But to do so, your mind must be absolutely clear."

"Clear?"

"Empty."

She then suggested I could ask the monkey for directions. So taking her advice, I asked. He said nothing and threw peanuts all over the place — she said at the four directions — and then seemed to point to the main building of the temple. At least that is how she interpreted it. So we went in.

Upon entering there was a small guardian temple to one side. Sheathes of arrows from ancient hunters and warriors were kept there. I looked at the cracked leather and oiled wood. They must have been hundreds of years old. The monks explained that certain hunters and warriors understood the pain others received from death created by their own hands. Deciding to stop hunting and fighting, they voluntarily brought their arrows and bows to Dromolakang over the years. Leaving them at the altar, they vowed not to kill again. These instruments of violence hung from the rafters of the protector temple, where dissipated incense gathered in fine clouds and then became dust. The monks explained that these discarded weapons represented how negative spirit had been transformed to protect the Tara within.

The monks at Dromolakang explained that the White Tara image had been lost and then found in the United States by a Chinese collector of antiquities who verified that it had come from this temple and returned it. The monks locked it inside a compartment within the altar so it would not be lost again.

Sure enough, this was the very White Tara that the great Indian master Atisha (982-1054 AD) had brought with him from India to Guge, and eventually here to the outskirts of Lhasa, where Atisha built Dromolakang and taught the Tara teachings until he passed away. These teachings then spread throughout Tibet.

Renzhen Deki mentioned in passing that if I really followed *Shambhala Sutra* literally as a guidebook, it would probably lead me to the vanished kingdom of Guge near the Kashmiri border in Tibet's remote western prefecture of Ngari. Many Tibetans aspired to visit this place, believing it represented the origin of Shambhala, a perfect harmonious Buddhist kingdom. It was the king of Guge who

had invited Atisha to Tibet as part of efforts to revitalize and revive Buddhism, which had at that time gone into a period of decline.

So in a way, I would be following Atisha's route backwards, she suggested. Then again, by following the sutra, I might eventually come full circle around. "There is nothing wrong ending up where you started," she offered with a shrug. "Cycles are always like that. They end at the beginning."

As the monk led us in, he explained, "White Tara has five eyes. They witness the suffering of humanity. There is so much suffering. She always holds one hand outstretched to help those who wish to be pulled out from the hell of their lives. But too many cry for her help."

I asked what White Tara embodied. The monk patiently explained, "When the Bodhisattva of compassion, Avelokitshavara, whom the Chinese call Guan Yin, cried upon witnessing the suffering of humanity, she shed two tears. One tear became Green Tara, who raises one hand to give refuge and places one foot upon a lotus taking a step toward action. The second tear became White Tara. On each of her hands, feet and her forehead are eyes to see the sufferings of all."

"What does this have to do with following *Shambhala Sutra*?" I questioned.

"It is important that you understand the powers of Tara before trying to follow the sutra if you really want to find Shambhala," Renzhen Deki injected, insisting that I understand. "Because it is true there are many demons on the way. They will haunt and hurt you. But you must understand that all demons can be subdued. The power to do this can be called upon by each of us inside, if we know how. That is why I brought you here. To find out."

Renzhen Deki then explained how within the Dromolakang Temple there are 21 different Tara statues. "We have a story about the Bodhisattva Tara. She has 21 manifestations. Once, these manifestations were all demons who tried to hurt her, being obstacles. One by one, she subdued the demons with her kindness and compassion. They in turn transformed from enemies to disciples, and then into her manifestations. This way they can help others when she is

too busy helping everybody else. That's why she needs 21 manifestations of herself. To overcome so many obstacles."

Sure enough, inside, 21 statues of Tara adorn both sides of the temple's inner sanctum. Renzhen Deki pointed to a crypt behind the altar, which held the tiny but sacred image of White Tara. "It is up to the monks whether to open the gate," Renzhen Deki advised. "Normally, they are reluctant because the image, although tiny, is overwhelming in her power, which is easily overlooked. So they rarely remove the figure. Because she is so tiny, most overlook her. But if you do not overlook, and listen carefully, she can speak to you."

"She can speak?" I asked, disbelieving. "You mean we can actually hear her speak?"

"Yes, if you listen very carefully," Renzhen Deki insisted. "But if you do not listen carefully enough, then how can you hear anything at all?"

A monk came back through the door into Dromolakang's inner sanctum. He carried an iron chain with keys clanging. Shifting a wobbly wooden ladder over to the crypt, he climbed up and with more clanging of keys, unlocked an iron gate protecting and secluding the precious White Tara. He then removed her, stepping down the ladder, slowly and carefully. The image, wrapped in colorful, delicate clothing is encrusted in layers of gold leaves. There are so many gold leaves that you cannot see the delicate features of her face or the tiny eyes upon her hands and feet.

The monk explained how White Tara once stepped from the crypt and stood in the temple. She then spoke. Everyone present at the time heard her voice, he assured me with conviction. Then pressing the tiny gold encrusted Bodhisattva to the top of my head, this monk added almost as an afterthought, "If you listen carefully, you too can hear her voice."

So I asked Renzhen Deki, "What are the words of a Bodhisattva supposed to sound like?"

She whispered in the softest of voices, "They sound like singing from afar, the call of a peacock in a distant valley, the cry of wind without the moon, and the chiming ripple of water trickling from mountain snows into vastness of the Lhasa River flowing just beyond the gates of Dromolakang Temple, which we are in right now. Listen. Can you hear her speak?"

Listening for a moment, I heard absolutely nothing. I asked why. The monk asked me to listen again. Renzhen Deki reminded me I was not listening carefully enough.

The Road

"To get to Shambhala you still
have a long road ahead."

Shambhala Sutra

"This has got to be the worst pizza I have ever eaten."

"It is my teahouse's most famous dish — yak meat pizza," Renzhen Deki stated with a hint of pride. "The cheese is from yak too!"

"I assume you created the recipe?" I asked.

"The Hindus in India have a saying: 'You are what you eat'. You have been living in Beijing and Hong Kong. By tradition, the Han Chinese eat pork. We Tibetans eat yak meat. Think about how both animals live their lives. Don't answer, just think."

Renzhen Deki poured another cup of yak butter tea. "So you should start getting used to eating yak. If you want to follow *Shambhala Sutra* to Mount Kailash in Ngari Prefecture, as His Eminence Beru Khyentse Rimpoche suggested, you must cross many mountain passes at over 5,000 meters above sea level. You have not done that yet, so you have not felt how thin our oxygen can really be. There are many such high passes on the road to Shambhala. You will have to cross each of them to get there."

"So drinking yak butter tea and eating yak meat will help fight off altitude sickness?"

"Yes." She responded firmly. "Do not underestimate our Tibetan ways. There is meaning and logic to everything we do."

"For instance?"

"See how we dress. Even in hot weather, Tibetans wear long thick robes, which are tied around our waists. The climate here can change abruptly. One moment, the sun will be bright and hot — wearing a t-shirt is warm enough. Do not be fooled though. Suddenly, rain will come or even snow with wind, and you will be caught unprepared. Even though it is summer, you need to take winter clothes wherever you go. The mood of weather can change abruptly. By the way, are you really going to go to Shambhala?"

"Yes."

"When will you come back?"

"I think in about a week or two."

"Are you so sure the trip will be so short?" She smiled, almost laughing.

"Why do you think this is so funny?"

Renzhen Deki opened the black box, removing the orange cloth-wrapped sutra and un-wrapped it. Fingernail touching the orange edges of faded paper, she turned the pages slowly, "It is old Tibetan, not so easy to read," she sighed. "But I can read some of this. And I don't think you should follow this and go there," she shook her head, looking at me through long strands of hair falling across her face.

"Why?"

"The *Shamhala Sutra* says there are a lot of demons along the way," She smiled, "What if they try to hurt you?"

"Maybe it's a problem. Do you have any suggestions? You already introduced me to a good Tibetan driver."

"Do you want to know what the sutra says?" she smiled. "It tells you how to cope with demons."

"Go ahead, read it to me. What does it say?"

"The sutra says, 'Cross a place without water or people. It is desert. Go for 21 days.' It describes this desert very clearly. The sutra says it is 'a place beyond a place where nobody has ever gone. But if you reach this place you must keep going because nobody has ever been there before'."

"What else does it say?"

"Have you ever thought about crossing a desert nobody has ever crossed before?" Renzhen Deki asked, ignoring my question by stretching her two curving eyebrows upwards. "Do you know what a desert is?" Without waiting for me to give an answer, she offered one. "It is the space in your mind between two echoes. Can you hear yourself when each echo stops? If you can, then maybe you have crossed the desert. Are you prepared to try?"

She was not waiting for an answer but had already heard it. She did not respond because she already had. I had not said anything; she had said everything. She did it with a simple smile and by pouring more tea.

"Ok. So what happens if I cross the desert? What does the sutra say?" I asked, sipping the hot tea. There seemed to be more yak butter than tea in the cup.

"After the desert, you will come to 'a place of tigers, snakes, angry animals and forest'. It says, 'travel for 12 days.' There are no McDonald's, Kentucky Fried Chicken, or even 7-11 chain convenience stores," she laughed. "In fact, there is nothing out there, not even a Sichuan dumpling stand. What will you do? If you can't eat the tigers, they will eat you!"

She put the sutra down and covered her mouth with both hands as if controlling a laugh. Then she could not control it anymore. The laugh seemed to go on forever. She stood up, walked across the room as if this was the funniest thing she had ever heard. I sat there sipping more tea. I would learn that Tibetans have an irresistible humor. Something very simple might seem uncontrollably funny, triggering enormous laughter. Each time this happened, I had to wait a long time for Renzhen Deki's laughter to dissipate into a giggle, before she returned and became serious again.

"Ok. So, what happens after the animals?"

She came back to the couch, sat down, and shifted through more orange edged yellow pages with her fingernail. She began to read the sutra again. "It says, 'You will then reach a place called *Genda* — a mountain with lots of medicine, flowers, trees.' There it says you will find 'a lion with eight legs...every day, he kills many animals. He is fierce'. But it also says, 'An angry animal can become kind. It can help you.' But here it tells you to 'kill the lion'."

"Why should I kill the lion? What's the point?"

"'The lion's blood can help you go to Shambhala', that's what it says".

"How can the lion's blood help me go to Shambhala?" To me, this seemed

 *Going*

to make no sense at all.

"The sutra says, 'Use lion's blood to draw a picture of a girl called *Mende Ha*. She is yellow with long teeth, and carries a yak skin bag with the blood and bones of animals in one hand and a sword of knowledge from the Bodhisattva Manjishuri in the other hand. She wears a skirt of human flesh. Put the animals killed by the lion before her. Meditate on her image and recite the mantra of Manjishuri 10,000 times, or until the demon goes away'."

"What's the mantra?"

"Om Ara Benzra Nadi."

"I have to recite that 10,000 times?"

"It would help. It is the mantra of wisdom. You will need it to find the right road."

"Better read me some more."

"*Shambhala Sutra* then says, 'Make hands like a bucket and talk to the demon'."

"What do I say to the demon?"

"It says the demon will ask you why you are going to Shambhala. When talking to demons, you should wait for them to ask questions first before answering," Renzhen Deki smiled, looking up through long strands of hair she quickly brushed from her face. "Didn't law school teach you how to talk to demons in a polite but effective manner?" I could see her white teeth through a smile — nomad teeth, pure, white like ivory. This time, she did not laugh.

"So if you are such a demonology expert, tell me how to talk to one."

"The sutra states," she said authoritatively, "just tell them: 'I am representing all sentient beings by going to Shambhala'."

"That's it?"

"That's it. The sutra tells you to say, 'I am going there for them'."

"That's all it says?"

"Not exactly..."

"What do you mean? It says something else?"

"No, not exactly either, sutras are not so clear like law books or even newspapers. You think everything in this world is black and white. But things are not. I know, where you come from, people just lead themselves into believing the world is this way. When westerners come to my teahouse, many ask about Tibet, about Buddhism, but don't really want to listen when I explain. They insist something is this way or that—the way they read about it in some newspaper or book. They are misleading themselves. They forget that black and white can be mixed and become gray. Sometimes gray is more beautiful, natural, cooling and soothing like the sound of rain. Actually, the color of rain is gray. Have you ever taken the time to listen to the color of rain?"

"No."

"Its color can only be heard by throwing out your umbrella and sitting in rain as it pours. Have you ever tried this before?"

"This sounds like a lot of bullshit to me."

"No, you are wrong. You do not understand."

"No. Everyone in Asia says to foreigners 'You do not understand' when we point out bullshit for what it is — bullshit."

She was clearly disappointed at what I said, and shook her head to show it. "You have to plead with the demon and ask, 'Can you help me on my way and not hurt me?' If you are sincere, the demon will say, 'Yes, I can help.'"

"Then what?"

"Then she will disappear."

"Just like that?"

"Just like that."

"Remember," Renzhen Deki implored, raising both eyebrows in yet wider arches, "each Bodhisattva has a wrathful manifestation."

"You mean a bad side?"

"Yes. Manjishuri carries a crystal sword. This Bodhisattva, the embodiment

of wisdom, when facing ignorance, becomes Yamantaka, with many arms and an angry yak's head devouring venomous snakes."

"So what's the point?"

"A Bodhisattva can become a demon. And a demon may be a Bodhisattva in disguise. So you should not overlook either," she smiled nodding. "Everybody changes with circumstance. Understand?"

"You seem to care a lot about this Bodhisattva stuff? Don't you?"

"Yes. My teahouse is the house of a Bodhisattva. Didn't you know? Or maybe you have not yet heard the story."

"What story?"

"The story of my teahouse. Would you like to listen to the story?"

She opened that small book on the table before her and began to turn the pages with long fingernails painted like a 60s flower child's. She came to a line and began to read, eyes shifting down upon the page with a concentration that seemed complete. "Many centuries ago, his Holiness the Sixth Dalai Lama used to sneak out of the Potala Palace at night. He was a romantic who loved to drink and sing. He wrote the most beautiful poetry in Tibet and we sing his poetry in songs today. Then one night, he came to this teahouse, the house we are in right now. He began to write poetry and sing. Suddenly from behind a curtain, he caught the glimpse of a beautiful young girl, whose charm entranced him at first sight. Convinced he had seen the Bodhisattva, White Tara, he returned to this teahouse almost every night, very late, searching for her. She never appeared again."

"Many tried to dissuade him from his search, suggesting he had seen a dream, just a momentary vision. He should give up looking because it would be futile. The girl must be only an illusion. They say the mind can play tricks. Have you heard of this? But the Sixth Dalai Lama always refused to believe these pessimists. That's why we Tibetans admire him so much."

"He returned to this teahouse again and again, especially late at night when the moon was full and the clouds were opened like lotus. He was always searching. In fact, he spent the rest of his life searching for this Bodhisattva, and they say he died for this quest. But do you want to know something? She never appeared again. He searched until his last breath of life."

Renzhen Deki finished telling the story. I was still drinking yak butter tea. The tall thermos that she kept pouring from, refilling my cup throughout the story, was still not empty.

"So do you still want to take this trip?" she asked.

At first I said nothing, lost on Bodhisattva information overload. Then I wondered out loud, "The demon in the sutra becomes a Bodhisattva and the Sixth Dalai Lama wrote a poem about a never-ending search for one? What's the point of all this?"

"You never know who you might meet on the road to where you are going, especially if you are not so sure where it will lead and why you came in the first place," Renzhen Deki poured more tea. "So be careful with whomever you meet, but always keep an open mind. That person could be a demon or a Bodhisattva, because you never know how they may change your life. It could be as simple as telling you where to go or just pointing in a direction. Only after you follow and get to where you never expected to be going do you realize how big an impact that person may have in changing the direction of your entire life."

"So what's the point?"

"Think of life like being in the Shambhala Palace described in this sutra. The palace has many doors. Each door leads in a different direction. The cause and effect linkages of stepping through each door will be different. By opening one door, you may meet different people, have different lovers and will die in a specific way at a certain place. If you open another and step through that door, then everyone you meet on the other side and everything that happens

will be different. How you live and die in this life determines how you will be reborn and live in the next. Remember, while each door is different, the road you follow once you step through, and everything that happens along the way, is linked and will lead to a specific outcome."

"So by walking into La Zha's shop and buying this sutra, I stepped through a door? Is that what you are saying?"

"Maybe. Soon you will be leaving for Ngari. When do you plan to go?"

"We're leaving tomorrow," I responded. "That Tibetan driver you introduced, Ge Ming, agreed to drive. I rented his jeep for the whole trip. He thinks it will take over 4,000 kilometers."

She said nothing for a moment. Then pointing at the thick incense stained orange adobe walls around her, she suggested almost as an afterthought, "When you return, just come here," she shrugged matter-of-factly. "Anyways, I am always here."

I thought about the trip ahead, listening to Renzhen Deki's firm but whispery voice. The road would be long. We needed to carry supplies, medicine, a tent, sleeping bags, extra films, packages of instant noodles, lots of toilet paper, and even gasoline in plastic containers. As I ran the checklist in my mind, I could see her reflection in the white milky tea. She asked, "Have you ever met a Bodhisattva in disguise?"

Returning

"Ok, your papers are in order," the border control soldier interrupted my thoughts with the assurance of somebody who was clearly in charge. In fact, he was the only one watching the gate. Ge Ming nodded, handing back both passport and the permission papers allowing us to cross into Ngari Prefecture. I put the papers back in my wallet, and stopped listening to the wind.

The soldier snapped his hands, waving us through with authority. A long iron pole painted in red and white lifted. It lifted ever so slowly. The wind was blowing.

We crossed the checkpoint. Entering Ngari, everything seemed so slow. I was breathing thin oxygen. It felt as if this had all somehow happened once before, maybe in a dream. Dust floated past on the tailspin of wind. I searched for a golden *hada* prayer scarf in the dust. It had already passed by.

On cliffs alongside the thin gravel composition serving as road were carvings of Bodhisattvas. One looked at me. She had white hands with eyes painted on them, and a third eye on her forehead. We passed the carvings. I thought about the eye on her forehead. Ge Ming interrupted my thoughts with his own, "After this checkpoint, you will need protection from all the Bodhisattvas in this place."

Throughout our several weeks on the road, this was the first assurance Ge Ming had said without assurance. He navigated our jeep gingerly through the checkpoint. "There is nothing after this place," he said definitively. Blue and yellow carvings of Buddha passed on my left, then another Bodhisattva image became smaller and smaller in our rearview window. Then it too disappeared on a horizon. I began to remember where we were going.

There was a distinct sense of crossing at an intersection. The cliffs bore open, revealing a vast space of grassland and desert. I could not see where grassland ended and desert began. Both merged into moonscape. The land felt as if it had once been the bottom of an ocean. Then somebody pulled a plug and all the water drained away.

Entering Ngari, I felt as if there was an abrupt break in my life. It was a deep feeling of distinct departure, as if falling into an irrational void.

Realization awakes illusion. No place ever was so vividly clear in my mind. I imagine returning to a desert I once visited in dreams. Ngari, a vast desert weaving into grassland, canyon and snow-covered mountains, possessed infinite unrestrained beauty and screaming absolute fear. Sharp pain struck a point behind the temple bone, piercing the veins behind my eyes. For a moment, short pulse echoes reverberated through my mind.

Entering Ngari erupted sudden awareness of a reoccurring dream — a place I had come to many times before but had not entered — and a desert that had not been crossed. Maybe I had already died here in other lifetimes and returned several times. Maybe I would die in it several times again before eventually decomposing into thin air.

In a flash, each previous dream reconstructed in my mind, like frames blinking on and off, rolling through a great projector in a movie theater. Having visualized the movie before, I knew it had just begun. Surety lost consciousness as our jeep rambled down the gravel path. I was entering my dream again. This was the one thing I was sure of.

Our jeep rambled silently, following a thin gravel corridor. It was the only path entering and leaving Ngari. During the weeks ahead, it was only the road ahead and the one behind. Desert spread before us. A sense of pervasive death spread into infinity. A lonely raven observed our movements. He cried. His voice resounded distinctly but left no echo. This time, I did not wake. It was time to return to a desert I had always been unable to cross.

Ngarí

"You will cross a place without water or people...It is desert...go for 21 days."

Shambhala Sutra

Ngari Prefecture is Tibet's most western and tightly restricted region. To most, it is inaccessible. Much of Ngari is no-man's land. The altitude is too high and the earth too harsh and desolate to support human life. So nobody lives there, except the nomads — Ngari is their land.

Nomads can live in Ngari. Here, they follow the contours of the earth by listening to the directions rivers flow in. The nomads of Ngari can survive here because they have learned to drift like the wind.

Such drifting is essential to survival. By drifting like wind, they avoid sharp sunlight when its afternoon rays cut like broken glass. Moving in shadows, they shift with the sun. The nomads understand the essential. They have learned to live off of it. And avoid what is unnecessary.

At any time in Ngari, you may find yourself crossing contours of land at 4,000-6,000 meters above sea level without realizing it. Snow-capped mountains rise above desert. Floating on horizons, they connect earth and sky. Everywhere in Ngari, there is the vast expanse of sky. It stretches — impenetrable blue in all directions — encircling you as you cross the desert.

By standing in the wind upon Ngari's desert, you feel as if you are about to dive into the sea. It is easy to lose directions. But in the sea you can swim. In Ngari you cannot, because it is a vast desert interlinking canyons of unimaginable proportion with the highest mountains in the world. Like entering a void within yourself, you enter Ngari.

The source flows from Ngari. The water of Asia comes from here. It flows from snow-capped mountains when glaciers melt in sharp summer sunlight. Summer sun pierces the ice frozen in winter when Ngari is abandoned by everything but the wolves. Snows melt in mid-summer flowing through the canyons. Across the plains, momentum pours into lowland rivers. Melted snow flows for a year before reaching the sea. It is the source of Asia's rivers.

Indeed, Asia's greatest rivers — the Brahmaputra, the Ganges, Yellow River, Yangtze and Mekong — all find their source from melting Tibetan snow. The origin of water for Asia's people comes from here. In a sense, the spirit of Hinduism, Buddhism and Taoism flow from these spirit mountains. The children of Asia are nourished on sacred water. You don't have to believe in anything mystic. But just think about it for a moment. It's their water.

In ancient times, people walked or rode horses across Ngari's desert to reach the sacred mountains. Nomads still do so today. Across the desert, snow-capped sacred mountains appear on horizons in all directions. In blazing late afternoon heat, they appear as floating mirages.

There is no sensible reason for all that white snow to be sticking out of the desert. At least that is the rational question, we think. Reach out to touch the mountains — they may be hiding behind the clouds. Follow the clouds into a sea of blue that cannot be grasped. It may appear purple. Enter the purple.

The only way to reach those mountains is to cross the desert by jeep. The road seems endless. In most places, there is no road. It will appear as two tire tracks of somebody who drove here first and maybe found their way, maybe not. The trick is not to get lost. Look for places where tall grass finally stops. That is where desert begins.

The desert goes on forever. Sometimes, it is rich red earth crawling with life tucked beneath stones. In other parts, it becomes sand dunes — so tall, they can drift and disappear before you can find them. Hidden behind the sand dunes are flat lakes like mirrors that reflect the clouds. Circle the lakes clockwise and follow the nomad pilgrims. They know where to go and can lead you to the other side of the lake. More deserts are on the other side. They too will need to be crossed to get to where you are going.

Just because nobody is here, do not delude yourself into believing that you came here first. There is always somebody who has already traveled this road.

They may have forgotten the way. We are only just re-tracing it, scratching deeper lines upon ones already drawn.

Look for carvings. They serve as clues. Traces of what we may have already seen at another time in our memories before somebody hacking into our brain system deleted it. Look for clues of what was discovered before. They may explain why we came here and why we left, or what to expect as we move on to the next place.

If unsure, ask the nomads who are passing. They never stay anywhere long enough to become complicated by illusions we cling upon to assure our permanency. They learned a long time ago that nothing is permanent. That is why they choose to be nomads. They do not buy insurance because nobody will insure them. That's why they keep moving.

By passing through this desert, follow a road others have taken, which some have forgotten, others have gotten lost, some have never finished. Their shadows are still here. But they are not. Some left the mantra Om Mani Bemi Hom carved on a rock — a reminder of their passing, and then left. They never returned or looked back. They had no regrets. Why? When sitting in the desert lingering on wind, they remembered to wait for the sun to finally stretch illusions into horizons before wandering to those horizons.

The path they followed stretches 5,000 meters above sea level. At this altitude, it is easy to believe the desert is just an illusion. It is only the outer skin of a canyon cutting below the surface, penetrating earth like a knife. Prick your skin and pretend that earth did not feel anything. Now try to cross the desert. It will become a canyon that can be entered. But by entering you can never leave. So is that why you entered?

Now at this point, frustration sets in. Directions seem undetermined. Do not worry. Do not be concerned. If lost, take the guidebook, tear it into pieces and throw them into the wind. Watch in which direction the torn pages blow.

Nobody really wants to continue and cross the desert. There are no mobile phone connections, or sockets to plug in to the Internet. The "Blackberry" will get caked with sand. None of the essential contraptions we use to define our reality works here. So it must not be reality. If we cannot get an international newspaper, maybe nothing worth reporting happened. If nothing was reported, did it happen?

Now please cut all the stuff about illusions and blowing dust. There must be timely stock market reports, oil derivative futures and currency quotes. If this desert is illusion and not reality, are passages blocked in our mind? But what if the desert is actually reality? Have we been blocking the passages?

The natural reaction is to get out of this place as quickly as possible. The fastest way is to backtrack the way entered — two tire tracks following movements of the sun. But having gone this far, do you really want to go back?

Beyond the desert, you must cross through mountain passes. Oxygen there is thin, making breathing difficult. At moments, you may feel vomit streaming from your stomach, leaving the throat dry. Actually, nothing had happened except a momentary shortage of oxygen to the brain. While death seemed to be creeping, it never arrived, because you felt widely awake.

Altitude sickness hits like this. It occurs in sharp gasps, if one tries to move fast. So move slowly. The pace of everything becomes deliberate. Things occur with a feeling as if nothing happened at all. That is why in Ngari, they never happened.

In Ngari, it is easy to forget things. Senses separate from body, caused by altitude — the thinness of oxygen dismantles thoughts from the senses. These are remnants of distilled moments already disintegrated. Definitions of space and time, they were units of events that have come and gone and are now scattered, left behind with your body, somewhere alone in the desert thinking by itself.

Remembering that it was, now forget where had you left it. Do not try to return to that place looking for your body. You cannot find it. This should not be a problem, so do not worry too much. Deliberately left where it was, it was meant to be forgotten.

A warning! Stop everything! Just leave it behind. Take all those things out of the box with a sense of finality and spread them before you on the desert sand like a deck of cards revealed before the game. Examine each of the cards carefully and remember to forget the numbers before the game begins. Wait for a moment and the wind will blow them all away. Now, it is time to cross Ngari's desert.

Adjust your breath according to the shifting direction of wind. Here, thinness of oxygen can best be seen by the physical eye when holding a thin golden *hada* prayer scarf to the blazing sun and then letting it drift into the breeze. It will vanish like a peacock in flight. It cannot be found again. This means the thinness of air in Ngari is non-existent. It is even thinner than light illuminated on the tip of a silk thread emanating from a prayer scarf lost in the wind.

When the wind's shadow finally disappears at a point where sky disintegrates into desert sands, distant horizons forget to be seen. The direction to follow will become clearer at dawn. So wait for dawn. It is the direction wind blows in the early morning light.

The waiting is so painful. It echoes that cringing cry of wolves at night when they have nothing better to do. If impatience sets in, follow the wind by chasing the laughter of ravens.

Here, in Ngari, ravens are so fat from picking at carcasses, they cannot fly very high. They fly low, drifting close to earth. By doing so, they have innately learned how precarious the direction of wind can be.

By listening to the wind for prolonged periods, it may echo in your mind like a resounding hammer. Some may dismiss the headache as altitude sickness.

Others may suggest it is the shattering of all things constructed in previous and current lives — the sudden crashing of assumptions.

This is the feeling of Ngari. The sound of wind penetrates all senses. It never leaves you. Feel the wind creeping across your skin, like the soft touch and breath of a lover you have never met. Even when wrapped and layered with sweaters, leather jacket and scarf, you can still feel her pervasive presence touching your skin with her tongue, because here, there is simply no way to escape the sound of the wind. Even by remembering not to listen to her, she lingers and will never leave. In Ngari, the wind is like that. It never stops. If it does, you feel cold.

Desert

"There is a place beyond a place where nobody has gone...
If you find this place, you must keep going because
nobody has gone there before."

Shambhala Sutra

Weeks had gone by without an e-mail or mobile telephone ringing. Even if I had one, it would be useless — in Ngari, there was no connection.

The process of disconnecting was like shattering a mirror. Things once considered important became meaningless. Trying to put pieces back together was useless. Leaving the mirror shattered on rocks, we drove into the desert.

"Permanence is unnecessary. You'd better forget rather than believe in it. If you start believing in it long enough, it is like looking into a mirror every day. You really think nothing changes. Actually, this is just an illusion like the reflection itself. Such a delicate thing as a thin piece of glass can be so easily shattered and dispersed into small, fractious sharp pieces that have no reflection at all."

I wrote this in the diary of my laptop computer on the second day crossing into the desert of Ngari Prefecture. After writing it, I threw out the laptop. Leaving it in the desert, we just drove off.

The guidebooks warn that anyone who tries crossing this desert will become crazy. It will affect behavior. It will strip everything unnecessary from your mind. This can be caused by exposure to excessive wind. It will blow away the dust.

Imagine looking at yourself in a mirror and then shattering it; Ngari's desert is like that. It does things like that to your mind. It takes everything we are taught to assume and believe and just shatters it. Looking to pick up the pieces is like searching for a computer in shifting sand dunes. When found, it is already useless.

This feeling is best understood when the sun rises. It feels hot and can burn your face. Tibetan nomads' cheeks are always like that — bright scarlet as if they have been pressed against the sun.

Their cheeks are red because nomads only expose their smiles without taking off their long, thick flowing robes, regardless of how hot the desert gets. They do not fear being hot but are afraid to be burned by the sun. In a way, their vast robes are like tents into which their bodies retreat into shade. They avoid the feeling of extremity and feel the cool in the shade.

So stay in the shade. By following the sun, assuredly you will go crazy. They warned you before taking this trip. It is written clearly, black and white in the guidebook next to the list of one star restaurants and home-stays to be found along the way.

A long road winding through dust and then more dust, then wind and sun will certainly make you insist upon arriving at the end of the earth. There is no way to stretch the imagination beyond this point except by staring at shadows on the horizon before sunset. There is nothing beyond the shadows except the horizon and that has already vanished with the sun. When you think about reaching there, it may be too late.

Don't you try racing with the shadows to catch the sun. When this happens, it is almost certain that complete madness has set in. It may be caused by a number of factors — dehydration, prolonged exposure to the sun, a lack of oxygen, or a faintness from altitude sickness for traveling over 5,000 meters above sea level. But do not worry. Prognosis is unnecessary. There are no doctors here in white jackets to prescribe what went wrong. There are no lawyers to analyze what the doctors did not do right. And there is no media to write about it, because there are no witnesses. So everything appears as if nothing had happened at all.

It is like listening to the sound of shattering glass without hearing it. That feeling of a complete taking apart of something fragile by simply shattering its totality is something you and I wanted to do every single day working in that office tower, but just could not. Imagine what people would say and think if we did?

Social order is like that — glass pyramids made of mirrors reflecting images that in reality are only refractions of themselves. Actually, the total make-up

of our social and economic reality is a kind of unreality given sanction because we do not really know what else to do with it.

We built it and cannot take it apart. So wouldn't it be nice to just break it? Maybe by doing so, we could start all over again. Isn't it about time we did?

Imagine all that shattered glass. It eventually splinters everywhere. Tiny fragments become so thin and intangible. If you put them under a jeweler's glass, they might appear to be fine diamonds waiting to be worn by a celebrity for some elegant event. Actually, when glass decomposes to this size, it is already returning to its original state, that of sand.

So imagine the celebrities arriving at a celebrity dinner wearing sand bags. That might be too much to think about, but there is a lot of sand here. It blows everywhere when the wind shifts. In fact, this whole desert is made of sand. So by entering the sand dunes, we see that the very structure we thought had been so carefully put together simply comes apart so easily. That's because it was never there in the first place.

After walking into the desert, the wind will cover your tracks. This means it is impossible to find the way back from where you came. So at this point, it is easy to become lost. Assured markers and familiar objects are only illusions. Easily assuming all directions were clear, you were actually lost even before arriving at this place without markers. It was the general direction of wind that brought you into the desert to begin with. So remember, if you never want to get lost, never forget to follow the wind.

This is what the nomads taught me. They hang prayer flags to observe its general direction and then flow with the momentum after the flags have blown away. They explained, offering tea beside a fire burning in the late afternoon, that the only way to be sure which way to walk is to follow shadows arising at a moment before the sun begins to set. The wind can clear the mind and bring it back to its totality. At that time, directions become momentarily clear.

So after sunset, run at night like a wolf in the clearness of white reflected by a full moon before the clouds arrive. Only when the moon is completely covered that darkness arrives. When it departs, the sun begins rising east and directions become clear again, but only for a moment. That moment is particularly important. It is the time to move on.

When the day grows upon you, realization sets in that the hottest time in Ngari is not midday but all afternoon, because when the sun crosses Ngari's desert, its rays fall like rain, forming rainbows without mist. They become kaleidoscopes in the recess of your mind, staying open and lasting until you sleep, only to dissipate when dreams become confused moments. This indicates that all directions are being blown into a sandstorm. The wind did it.

Pour water into the sand and watch it disappear. This is simpler than trying to observe a rock grow. Maybe it is a fast track to meditation. So do not stare at the rock too long or the ravens will think you have gone crazy. They will fly in all directions, making noise until it becomes clear that you have to move on. Keep moving.

Suddenly, realization occurs that all the time, money and frustration spent buying so much stock and saving for so long are actually for nothing. The global economic modules we had been taught to believe in become irrelevant. That was not supposed to happen. But here, everything becomes reduced to the simplest of conclusions. That big house everything was mortgaged for, when you die, will be empty and no different from this desert.

It is in places like the desert that our minds are actually allowed to be uncluttered and start thinking, or maybe questioning this entire arrangement. The desert does that to you. It deletes all that stuff in the e-mail inbox of our minds.

Imagine a box of old broken toys in a child's room. The child has grown and is interested in other things. But nobody bothers to throw away the toys. They just continue to fill the box. Do not throw away the toys! Take the box of toys and give them to orphans. But remember to bring back the empty box. Now it can be used to collect something new. We can do something meaningful with that as well.

Now I know what you are going to say at this point, this stuff about empty boxes and orphans is just nonsense. You were thinking that, right? All this UNICEF stuff is for NGOs, right? Nobody has time to think about emptying boxes when we have to worry about filling them. GDP growth, stock market indexes, the kind of cars our colleagues are buying to fill their garage, or the universal values which have been determined by G-8 at the World Economic Forum, are the things which make the world economy go around.

All this stuff about boxes being overstuffed is irrelevant unless you are a monk, a vegetarian, or taking a yoga class. Is that what you are thinking? I knew it! That's alright. Just calmly write down the thought as a message on your "Blackberry" without misspelling anything, and then just send it. It does not matter who you send it to. Just send it. Now that we've done that, let's begin again.

Think of a satellite dish. Radio electronic magnetic airwaves pass from antenna to dish. This function succeeds because the dish is empty. That is why it is called a receiver. It can receive. If it is full of unnecessary static, if the satellite dish looks like a Chinese wok full of stir-fry, then it is overfilled with turbulent static and chili oil, making reception impossible. So for our minds to function as a receiver, it must be empty.

When one starts thinking like this, they will assure you, everything is over. You have lost it. There is no excuse. Warnings were written all over the guidebook. They were very clear, delineated in bold print. Even early evening cocktails at the club will not be able to save you. Imagine. You have lost interest in shopping, stock market reports and sports news. So there is nothing left to talk about. You have finally lost touch with reality. The psychiatric analysts will throw their

hands up in the air in despair because the insurance companies won't pay their bills any longer. Then you must be through.

There is really no point trying to bring you back. This is because you have finally arrived at the place called 'a point of no return.' Remember, they warned you about this in the guidebook. It was all written clearly, everything explained. Did you check the glossary in the back before leaving? That point was described in concise terms. It is defined as the line drawn in sand before crossing the desert.

Lakes and Mountains

"There is a big lake. Water is white in color and very cold, so cold it flows to hell, so cold it cannot become ice but it is colder than ice. Whoever touches it will be burned...So go around the snow mountain. There are many people practicing meditation there."

Shambhala Sutra

We had come to Poison Lake. Here the car broke down, maybe because of the poison in the lake, maybe because there was too much sand in the carburetor. Ge Ming opened the hood.

I opened *Shambhala Sutra*, asking him to stop fixing the car and help read a passage. He read it, "Near the place where nobody has gone, there is a huge lake called Tsi Dai. If you touch the water, your finger will rot instantly. Nobody can cross this lake."

"So this must be poison lake. What do you think?"

"Actually, the lake is not called Tsi Dai, but Tok Chok," he said with a disregarding shrug. Then he thought for a moment. "Actually, in Tibetan '*tok*' means poison and '*chok*' means lake. The truth is, this lake has too much alkaline," he explained. "The water cannot be drunk, and you can't swim in it either. The acidic levels are too low. We'll have to take the road around," he conceded.

Here, we stopped the jeep at a place where sand dunes lead to lakes. There is absolutely no reason for the lakes to be beside the sand dunes. In the desert, there should be no lakes; otherwise, it is really not what you expect to find in the desert.

But this is Ngari, a place of juxtapositions. It shatters preconceived notions of what should be where and what should not because everything has been moved around like a child in a playroom who takes all the toys apart and puts them back together incorrectly. It is never bothered by adult preconceptions of what the right way should be, because nothing was ever really any particular way to begin with.

Lakes here are like that too. They have been placed in juxtaposition with each other. This lake is a good place to take a deep breath and drink another mouthful of water, or fill up a thermos. Some lakes here have water so pure that you can

be enlightened just by drinking it. Others have water that is poisonous. It does not make sense, when one thinks about the proximity, of their differences.

We came upon Demon Lake after a few hundred kilometers more. People talk about kilometers like that in Ngari. "Oh, that place is not far, just another 300 to 500 kilometers away." For a Tibetan driver like Ge Ming, it is nothing. Crossing 500 kilometers in his mind would be like driving to a nearby grocery store for a quart of milk or a newspaper. In Ngari, after a while one just begins to think about distances like that.

The Tibetans call it Demon Lake. It is always covered in black clouds. One cannot stay here very long because it is cold and often raining.

No fish can live in Demon Lake. Maybe it is due to high salt or alkaline content. But Tibetans explain it differently. They say the lake is associated with Mahakala, a favorite protector spirit of Tibetan people. He often appears with six arms carrying weapons, a big furious face with gnashing teeth, a protruding tummy and two solid feet standing on an elephant-headed human corpse, symbolizing his trampling and crushing of ignorance.

But Mahakala also has an originating connection with Ma-ha-kali, or Kali, the

Indian goddess of destruction from which the Kali Yulga or 'Age of Destruction' arises.

Shambhala Sutra describes, "Here, the people around this lake are committing many terrible things — terrorist activities." While everything at Demon Lake seemed pretty quiet because nobody was there, the connection with Kali appeared clear. So somewhere following the trail of Kali, we should arrive upon Shambhala. At least that's what I thought. That's what the monks said. Shambhala comes after Kali.

Right beside Demon Lake, over a slightly grassy mound not quite a hill but bigger than an incline, is another body of water called Spirit Lake. The two lakes lie in almost Yin-Yang proximity. The water is clear and fresh. Tibetans say that flying angels once brought Buddha's mother here to wash her womb before his birth. The water is that pure. And the lake is full of fish.

Shambhala Sutra describes Spirit Lake as well. "Beside the lake are many caves. In the caves, you will find many meditating hermits. There is no way to cross the cold water."

"Are there hermit monks here?" I asked Ge Ming.

"Actually, they are always here. But you cannot be sure to meet them. But there is one thing you can be sure of. They do not want to meet you. This is the nature of hermit monks. They become hermits because they want to be alone."

In explaining this, Ge Ming pointed to another passage in *Shambhala Sutra*. "'There are Indian masters who can go around the world many times in a lifetime. They just go everywhere.'" He explained, recalling from another trip, "I once met an Indian yogi who had stayed here for some time." He added, "Actually, a lot of Indians come here to visit Spirit Lake, Demon Lake and in particular, Mount Kailash. We can see a lot of hermits, especially at Mount Kailash. It is sacred to both Hindus and Buddhists."

Surprised, I asked why it was sacred to both.

"Mount Kailash is the most sacred mountain in the world," Ge Ming pronounced with pride. For Hindus and Jains, it is the abode of the god Shiva. For Tibetan Buddhists, it is the place where the great yogi Milareapa practiced meditation. Some Buddhists feel it represents Mount Meru, the central naval of our universe. In a way, this makes a lot of sense. Four great rivers flow from its snows — the Indus, Brahmaputra, Sutlej and the Ganges."

Then looking at the sutra, Ge Ming pointed to another line, "Shambhala is north of Mount Meru. Our world is south." These lakes are directly south of Mount Kailash. We can reach Kailash by tomorrow."

Many pilgrims circumambulating Kailash begin their *kora* by visiting a celestial burial altar. There, they will look for bodies or body parts not yet eaten by the white eagles. They will lie on the altar beside the bodies and sometimes roll themselves among them. This is because they know that when death occurs, their body may be far from Kailash. However, they wish for their souls to remember clearly how to return to the mountain.

At a Tibetan celestial burial ground, nothing is memorialized. There are no signs, plaques, sarcophagus or stone crosses. In fact, nobody is buried here at all. It is an altar upon which bodies are presented to white eagles. Here, everyone is equal. Only clear blue sky is unequal, because like the sea, it cannot be grasped or held. Reach out to touch it with both arms, and the sky will run away and laugh at you from above. It is always there, a penetrating crystal blue. Aside from blue, there is only blue.

As our jeep drove across the plane toward Kailash, Ge Ming told me about the celestial burial altar. When we arrived at the altar, marked by a pole with prayer flags blowing in wind, he began to talk about death and dying.

"For us Tibetans," he explained, "We prefer a sky burial. Look, the burial ground is always clean, nothing left. Everything has all been eaten by the white eagles (these are vultures, known to the Tibetans as 'white eagles') and taken away. Giving our flesh to the white eagles is a last act of kindness. Imagine

yourself hungry for a few days with nothing to eat. Then somebody comes along and gives you a piece of bread. You will be very happy too. It is like that for them. They will be very happy. So we give our bodies to them. Life then ends as a full cycle of compassion. But when there are no bodies here, you do not see the white eagles. That is because they fly very high."

I thought about a sky burial. Sitting on the massive slab of rock forming the sky burial altar at Mount Kailash, I tried calling to the white eagles — wanting to speak with them to understand their thoughts. They ignored me —probably they did not want to fly low and stop for a moment to have a conversation.

White eagles eat and carry flesh to the furthest reaches of imagination. They are just so good at this, serving as messengers darting between earth and sky. They believe that chasing the wind is an art few have attained. It can only be learned at high altitudes.

The white eagles come to feast on disregarded bodies. They present flesh to snows of Kailash as offering. Only white eagles remember how to fly to the place of offering. But when you ask them where the flesh was placed, they pretend to forget and fly in different directions. This is not an act of confusion but one of defiance. Actually, they do not want to tell you. Sometimes they laugh, because they have already eaten the flesh.

A Spirit

"Use blood to draw a picture of a girl...she has
the sword of Manjishuri in one hand and
wears a skirt of human flesh.
Meditate on her image...Tell her, 'I am traveling
to Shambhala for all sentient beings'...then cross
the river...in this place there are no people..."

Shambhala Sutra

Before the symmetrical white pyramid of Mount Kailash, a wide stone slab juts parallel across the basin of a valley. This is the first point on the pilgrimage route around Kailash. The stone slab is a celestial burial altar.

Here, bodies are brought and lamas dissect and feed them to the white eagles. This is considered a last act of compassion by each human being, to allow your body to be feasted upon by the white eagles. They descend from clouds. They bring you back with them when they leave.

I met a girl at the celestial burial altar. She had a long forlorn face framed in thick black hair tied in knots above her head, and wore chunks of blue turquoise in her hair the way nomad women do. Her face beamed with a simple kindness of the Tibetan plateau, where yak butter tea and fresh yogurt is offered to strangers arriving at a nomad tent. They have no knowledge of who the strangers are; they do not ask any questions and nobody asks for money when the strangers leave.

The girl was about my age. She had large eyes and a sad expression. When I first met her, I assumed she had children, but was not really sure. It was only a feeling. We talked for several hours. Actually, we did not speak at all; she was no longer there.

She had arrived the previous day. Her whole family had come, children as well. They remained for a while and left. She stayed and then left.

It was only after she left that I found her. The blood was fresh under my feet. It settled in crevices and cracks of the celestial burial altar, a sheer slab of stone jutting horizontally from the side of Mount Kailash. It extended like a knife, from the side of the mountain. It was flat and wide, a perfect natural spot to place many bodies before the snow-capped vision of Kailash.

It was freezing but the blood remained warm. It glistened in small patches caught between crevices, places where stone was split by wind and rain. Here it settled, purple in color, catching the movement of sun reflected like a mirror against Mount Kailash's sheer white face. Feeling fresh blood warm against cold, I followed the blood.

Then I found her plastic identity card. It was first issued by the local Public Security Bureau of the place she had come from, when she was just eighteen years old. It had been re-issued with an updated photograph when she was older, and then again after that. Now the plastic identity card was caught between two pieces of wild grass about to be blown in the wind. I picked up her identity card and read it. Her photo was black and white. She stared at me through her photo. Awareness crept in from the mountain. Nothing was left of this girl, except her identity card.

I was confused for a moment, wanting to write down her name and identity card number. But she did not want me to. I could hear her voice. She asked me not to write these things down. They were unnecessary. Her family had already left her here. That was all she had wanted. They had not kept anything, so why should I? In fact, I never even knew her. The information was not needed to fill a notebook, a computer, or a digitized serial base. One day, statistics would all be irrelevant anyway. All these things will ultimately be deleted. So writing anything down, she felt, would be unnecessary.

Instead, I placed her identity card under a rock, so that it would not be blown away. Maybe that was too much an act of permanence for such a place as Kailash's celestial burial altar. I did not want it to be blown away by the wind as if nobody cared. Somehow, that seemed too impermanent. But actually, placing it under a rock could not help her at all.

She reminded me there was no reason to hold on to either her name or her identity card number. It would be simply enough to place her plastic identity card under a rock, and to remember to forget where it was.

She was gone. I reached out and looked for her, but could feel only strands of hair, braided and long beside her clothes — scraps torn to shreds by the white eagles where they had been feasting.

I called upon the white eagles to ask where she had gone. One flew above from the mountain. He called tauntingly, as if to remind me that my flesh would be eaten too, sometime very soon. "Just close your eyes for a second. When you open them, your life will be gone as well," he laughed. "Then we can have another feast."

I asked the eagle where she had gone. He did not answer but continued to fly higher, reminding me that she was no longer here. White eagles never descend to earth, he explained, but only to the sky burial altar. It is a high cliff. They bring flesh and bone from cliff to sky. From here, they can fly higher.

So I placed her identity card under a rock and then began looking for her things. They were all there, where the white eagles had left them. Plastic bracelets lay scattered. The white eagles are careless with these things.

So I asked the white eagle to tell me what had happened the day before. It recalled the feast. High lamas had disemboweled her with thick axes and blunted knives. They shattered her skull with a large round stone. It was so large that three lamas were needed to lift the stone. It was very good for smashing skulls and had smashed countless ones before. In fact, it had shattered so many skulls that it had been smoothed by the sound of cracked bones. The white eagle pointed to the stone. It sat in a pool of blood.

Afterwards, the high lamas summoned the white eagles to feast, calling each one carefully by its name. Just a bare whisper was required. Each white eagle at a celestial burial ground has a name and its own distinct personality. Some like to eat a lot; others have trouble with digestion.

The white eagles are keepers of this place. They know the lamas and can read their inner moods when not frightened by the sounds of death and sadness of those who miss a soul when it has departed. When the sadness leaves, souls cling to the lamas' robes because they do not know where to go. That is until the white eagles come. They listen for their names to be called. One day, they will even eat the lamas who now feed them.

The white eagles descended, clawed and cut at the internal organs. The moon turned green. They eat the flesh and drink the blood. Bones which are cracked, ground and mixed with mashed barley taste sweet. The white eagles return for the bones. Sucking marrow into their veins, the nutrition nourishes, and their feathers become white like soft crystalline snows of Kailash. Once they had finished eating, they fly back to Kailash. Their feathers drift with the snows.

Like shadows of white silk, they can be seen within the inner remote thoughts of lamas meditating on the face of Kailash when changing wind blows prayer flags in uncertain directions. They can see what happened to the young woman

as well. The white eagles ate everything, except some scraps of clothes and braids of hair. But her plastic bracelets could not be eaten — they played with them instead. When finally bored, the white eagles left these colored bracelets in pools of blood soaked into crevices of the rock.

The white eagles were here first. Then they flew away in four directions. Taking pieces of flesh others had forgotten, they brought them to the wind. Do not try to follow the wind. It will mislead you into believing in the permanence of your own soul and this will only bring confusion, and ultimate disappointment.

I found her plastic bracelets. They were many different colors — purple, green, violet and blue. Shiny and new, she must have bought them not too long before she died. Maybe they were the most expensive possessions she had. Maybe they had no value at all. They had been scattered, but remained in one area. There were strands of her hair, braided and long, and scraps of clothes. A wooden drinking bowl for yak butter tea lay on its side. These bowls were often given to Tibetans when they were born. Sometimes, they carried them throughout their entire lives. Her blood was still fresh upon the rocks. As we spoke, I could still smell her breath, alive in the blood oozing from her voice.

We sat together for a moment and she drank yak butter tea from the bowl she had used since childhood. She told me about her life wandering across the plateau. She remembered a nomad tent she lived in as a child, where dark smoke from yak dung filled the air, warming it against frosty winds drifting like a hurricane across the plateau.

Nomad life was tough. She later moved to a village, married, then had many children. There were sadness, pain, happiness and then a disease. She had been sick for some time; the cough was acute. She asked for little, only to hold her children one last time. Afterwards, she asked to be presented to the white eagles at the sky burial altar beside Mount Kailash.

It was a long pilgrimage, which her family had no money for. But nevertheless, her family saved some money and brought her to Kailash. Then they left. They

returned across the grasslands and mountains to where they had come from, places she had lived, laughed as a child, cried as an adult. She never saw them again, because she had begun to be eaten by the white eagles. Thoughts turned to the white snows of Kailash.

After recalling this, she finished drinking her tea. Anyway, it had already evaporated in the frosty cold caught in rays of early autumn sun. Then placing the wooden bowl to its side, she left. I thought about our conversation for a moment, strained to remember everything. Then I tried looking for her, thinking it might be possible to bring her back. But she was already drifting with the snow.

The Epic War

"There are many demons and horrors ahead.
But if you read the sutra many times you can overcome them."

Shambhala Sutra

"So all of this counting of stratum by geologists in canyons like the ones we've been driving through is irrelevant?" The canyon of Tulin seemed enormous. I thought maybe five Grand Canyons could easily fit in it. We drove further, dropping eons as the red gravel road winded, descending.

"There is no point even trying an attempt to measure the age of our planet," said Ge Ming matter-of-factly. Rather, the idea of trying to define a time sequence, eons and epochs, seemed pointless to him. All these layers just served to remind us that our very existence is really just reduced to one of the tiniest, most finite fractions of time imaginable. As a Tibetan, he already understood this intrinsically.

"Think about all those layers of stone, once sediment under the sea, and the universe around us," he nodded at the red canyon stratum on both sides. "Our universe is only a small corner of countless other ones out there."

"So what you are saying is our lives are only as short and meaningless as an insect's, born in the morning and dead by night? At the end of the day, everything we do is irrelevant because in reality nothing ever happened. Right?"

"Ask yourself this question after reaching Guge," said Ge Ming.

The ruins of this lost kingdom of Guge, Tibet's Troy, had just disappeared. Nobody knows why. There are lots of stories — epic war with Kashmir being most likely — I asked which one was true.

"These stories mean nothing unless you have been there," Ge Ming insisted. "After you arrive, they will mean even less, because then you will begin to understand the meaning of Guge."

One approaches Guge from the desert. It rises like a precarious pyramid from the bottom of Tulin's red rock canyon. Walls throughout the canyon have caves dug out, clearly remnants of dwellings now gone, which flanked the kingdom's center, early satellite cities.

What most people think of as Guge, reproduced on postcards and in photo albums sold throughout Lhasa, is actually only just the temple and palace complex built into the side and on top of a mountain. Those images were just the center of a vast megalopolis kingdom. It once spread throughout Tulin canyon.

In *Shambhala Sutra*, there is a description of Shambhala Palace, a complex of interlocking windows and doors filled with bright lights on top of Mount Meru. It is the center of the Buddhist cosmos, from which the eye can see in all directions — four continents surrounded by water and rings of snow-capped mountains — fire and wind below. To reach Guge, we had crossed snow-covered mountain passes, interlocking rivers, vast lakes and flaming hot desert. Wind, of course, was everywhere.

I began thinking about what Nyima Tsering said about entering a *mandala*, taking it apart and putting it back together. The first ring was wind, followed by fire, water, earth, and Mount Meru. On top of the mountain is the Palace of Infinite Light. Was Guge the kingdom of Shambhala?

I was in the process of trying to take everything already taken apart and putting them back together in my mind when the silhouette of Guge rose in the early morning sunlight. We crossed an incline with red earth spitting from beneath our jeep tires.

It seems the central government complex of Guge was also built in a ring formation. Dwellings for the military officers were at the foot of the main mountain. They were protectors of the ancient kingdom. Homes for nobility were on the next levels. Temples lay in the central sections, with the king's palace right at the top.

My first impression was a question: In those days, did politics rule religion top-down, or did religion serve as the base upon which politics obtained credibility to rule? Then I thought about a second question: What about today?

Walking up a winding narrow dirt path, it seemed that everything in Guge was

eroding. Ruins of the ancient kingdom resembled a melting ice cream castle.

Entering the darkness of a temple, my eyes adjusted to light filtering through rooftop windows touching murals unlike any I had ever seen before. They seemed to represent a fusion of Kashmiri and Nepalese, Mogul, even Iranian style that had somehow in their convergence become distinctly Tibetan.

I found myself staring, or being stared at, by statues of Bodhisattvas facing inward into the large hall from all directions, their arms broken during rampages of the Red Guards who in their fervent, had made it across Ngari's desert and mountains to Guge. Now in the era of new Chinese capitalism, when greed and money worship overwhelms all ideals and beliefs, antique dealers were continuing the desecration, this time for money, not ideology. The damage seemed no less.

In a corner of this vast temple sat a thin man with a mustache and half a beard, wrapped in cigarette smoke. For a moment, I almost mistook it as incense rising in the light filtering at sharp angles from the rooftop.

"These murals are over 900 years old," he uttered in a scratchy deep voice, blowing rings of cigarette smoke. Han Xinggang stepped over from a mural he was delicately repairing. He took another puff. Smoke covered his mustachioed face hidden under long hair and a baseball cap.

Alone with a Tibetan colleague, Han Xinggang had spent 20 years working in Guge. Aside from restoring murals, he painted precise reproductions to be retained as records of these treasures in the National Bureau of Cultural Relics in Beijing. Despite this painstaking work, there was suspicion and even fear that most of these one-of-a-kind reproductions had been sold off by Beijing officials to private collectors.

We commiserated over the possible futility of a lifetime spent saving remnants of a precious culture which Chinese officials felt could, like everything else, just be sold for fast money. I realized Han himself had almost become like a monk, dropping everything in life to sit alone in Guge's isolated temple

complex, meditatively and caringly restoring and preserving something with his heart. It is a job that would never be appreciated by most. Han must have felt bewildered in the futility of his work, and even abandoned.

"Of course you feel abandoned. This place is abandoned," I remarked. "Nobody is here? Not even Tibetan people? Why?"

"They fear it," he explained, inhaling more cigarette smoke. "People are still afraid to come here to the ruins of Guge."

"Why?"

"They wish to avoid what they fear." He blew smoke into a trickle of light emanating from the rooftop. Aside from light creeping into the dark temple from its wide doors outside, this was the only light that cut through darkness. It lit half his face. The other half was covered in smoke. "The reason for this kingdom's destruction remains a mystery," he said with another puff. "They do not know why it happened. People fear what they do not know."

Han recalled when he first arrived in Guge. "Of course, there was nobody here, everything abandoned. Only an old watchman named Mai Waidui. For years, he was the only person the government assigned to watch over and guard the ruins of Guge. This place was just too isolated. And in those days, nobody came here. So it seemed that one watchman might just be enough to guard the ruins of this vanished kingdom."

"It must have been frightfully lonely being by himself in these vast ruins," I wondered out loud, searching the darkened halls around me.

"No mistake, it was a lonely job," Han sighed and shook his head, recalling his friend, now passed away. "But Mai Waidui did not mind. He had come to feel almost like a part of the ruins himself. In fact, he could not leave."

"Why not?" I asked. "Was it because in those days there was no jeep or trail to take him out?"

"No." Han shook his head amidst halos of cigarette smoke. "The truth was," he whispered, "the headless solider refused to let him go."

"Excuse me," I interrupted. "Did you say 'headless soldier'?"

"Yes," Han went on, undisturbed by what he had just said. "When Mai Waidui first arrived in Guge, he slept in a shack built alongside the ruins. When the moon was black and the wind dissipated into dust, he could hear in his sleep the sound of horses crying in the dark. That was when he awoke, but he was not sure whether he had or not. In his dreams, he saw the door of his shack open, allowing the sound of wind to enter and fill the space warmed by a kerosene flame, still flickering from the evening before. Suddenly, it went out."

"Then what happened?"

"He reached out into the space around him, but it was just darkness. Then he saw a headless soldier standing over him. Of course, Mai recognized the armor — small pieces of steel sewn together like a net of chain mail. That is what they wore as armor in the days when the kingdoms of Guge and Kashmir were at war."

"So what did Mai do?"

"He awoke," Han explained slowly. "He understood the message. Sometimes, messages come like that — half dream, half reality. If you are not sure it is a dream, then it may be reality. Most of the time, we live in reality, but it is just a dream. So when messages like this arrive, they are very real. At least, they should be listened to."

"Then what was the message?"

"The headless soldier opened the door and spoke to Mai Waidui, asking him to stay and guard. So he could not leave. From that point on, Mai believed his life's duty had been fixed — to watch over the ruins of Guge. He remained in this job for years. But the cost of this was he dreamed of war and killing every night. The horrible scenes that had taken place in these ruins during the downfall of Guge re-ran in his subconscious dreams like a movie, even though he himself had not lived through it. But living here, he could see it repeated every night. He had to watch and re-watch it. In the end, he drank a lot during the day. He hoped it would help him sleep at night. But it did not."

"That's pretty strange. It was like that until he died?"

"Yes. Other strange things also happened during those years. There was a huge raven. He stayed here. As travelers began to make their way to Guge, the raven warned us on each occasion when a tourist jeep arrived. He would call out, flying above before anybody else could see dust from jeep tracks rising in the distant desert. One day, an American tourist sporting a bird gun arrived. He tried to kill the raven. The American succeeded in shooting down the raven. He was very pleased with himself and left. But after he left, the raven returned."

"This place has a bit of mystery to it," I wondered out loud.

"Of course," Han exclaimed. "The whole place is a mystery. To this day, no archeologist can explain it."

"What do you mean?"

"The problem is, when this kingdom was abandoned, there were no survivors,

128

no descendants or even records to explain what really happened here. No one knows how the kingdom met its demise."

"I heard most of what is known about Guge has been passed through songs or oral stories? Is that true?"

"Yes. There are songs that tell of the Tuolin Monastery and life along the river. But now the people who settle in this valley have no relation with its past. We do not believe they are actual descendants of the original Guge people. Certainly there has been a break. The original descendants of Guge may have wandered out of this valley and headed toward Kashmir. Clearly, the descendants of the original inhabitants of Guge are not here. So many specific things we have uncovered cannot be linked to any answer, because there is nobody who can explain it. Some things have been passed orally through songs left behind. They provide hints but not answers."

"Buddhism was the central force sustaining this kingdom for so long." I asked, "Then why did it go into decline?"

"Guge was a powerful center of Buddhism," Han replied. "Very early, in 90 A.D., the Nyingmapa were ascendant. The king supported this sect. Then the Kadjupa, Kalupa all came here. Even though this place is remote, it became a center for religious activity. Differences between different Buddhist orders arose as they debated philosophical interpretation. Court politics became complicated. But the kingdom was very prosperous. Then things began to fall apart in 1630, not because of rivalry between different Buddhist sects, but due to Catholicism from the west."

"So then how did the kingdom collapse?"

"Definitely, there was war. Many speculate as to what happened and different versions are often re-told until people take it as truth. So you cannot believe when people tell you something assuredly about this place and say it is a fact. Different records remain but they do not provide us with enough specific details to formulate any scientific explanation. Because we have little to serve as basis,

we are stuck piecing together bits of a puzzle. Certainly rivalry existed between the different Buddhist sects — Nyingmapa, Kagyupa and Gelukpa — and they jostled with one another for influence over the court. But decline really occurred after Catholic missionaries converted the queen. She influenced the king and he converted to Catholicism as well."

"So destruction of the kingdom was then precipitated by religious infighting?"

"During the course of this prolonged rivalry, the Kalupa order became ascendant at Tuolin Monastery down the nearby valley. Influence of the monastery increased while power of the palace waned and faded. Local people were actually opposed to Catholicism and the palace's conversion. Nevertheless, the king tried to force Catholicism on his people. The rigidity of doctrine and intolerance for other ideas could not be accepted. So in reaction, the people began turning against the court."

"Then what happened?"

"It is said that the king of Kashimir then launched massive attacks on Guge. Some say it was to protect Buddhism against Catholicism. Whether the Kashmiri king's motivation was really to eradicate Catholicism or for some other ulterior reason — maybe even avenging a past diplomatic slight between the kingdoms — it remains today uncertain why he launched the war. These could have all been excuses for what might have been a broader strategic interest. Who knows? There are too many different versions and explanations."

"What is yours? What do you think really happened?"

"Hard to say," he coughed and for a moment, his face was lost in smoke. "But one fact is clear. In 1630, an epic war erupted, and this kingdom of Guge was annihilated. Guge as a kingdom disappeared due to religious infighting and war. When one ideology competes with another for supremacy, only destruction will result. After ransacking Guge, the Kashmir troops then abandoned this entire place."

"Why?" I asked. "If the kingdom was so rich, why didn't they stay and occupy it?"

"The reason is really not so difficult to understand if you think about it clearly," explained Han, taking another cigarette from the pocket of his blue shirt. "This entire kingdom spread as a network of interlocking canyon civilizations. Because each canyon had water sources, people could retreat deeper into the canyon and still live very easily. They could retreat into even more remote canyons, regroup and come back. So, for any occupying army to control the kingdom, even after smashing its capital, would prove very difficult. Moreover, occupying it would be too costly to sustain."

"So really, the Kashmiri army faced the same problem as today's occupiers in Afghanistan and Iraq?"

"It is one thing to win a quick war; another to occupy a territory like this which is not your own. Controlling this region did not make economic sense, so an

external force could not just come in here, occupy, and hope to sustain rule."

"So after the fall of Guge, the population of the original kingdom continued to live here?"

"Archeological evidence does reveal that there was once an extensive population living here, certainly much greater than today. It is also possible that people continued living here until as late as the early twentieth century. The place witnessed its final collapse around that time. At least this is the explanation that a 70-year old man gave us. He did not talk about war but disease."

"What disease?"

"The old man said that people here once had a practice or a custom. Every year around July or August, they would go to a snow mountain near Zhada called Gamei. Near that mountain was a village. Every year, people from Guge and that village met there. It became a kind of tradition. They met at the bottom of the mountain, sang songs, wished each other well for the year ahead, and exchange rocks. The last time this occurred was at the end of the nineteenth or early twentieth century. When people here went to the snow mountain to sing and exchange rocks, they did not know that most people in the other village had already died. So, in keeping with tradition, they sang and exchanged rocks with the survivors, but did not realize the rocks they brought back had already been contaminated."

"So it was pestilence, not war, that ultimately led to Guge's final collapse?"

"The old man explained that shortly after the pestilence spread, the people died quickly one after another. Only the strongest survived. There was no cure. The monastery was in horror, convinced that a demon had struck. They took the bodies to a cave by the riverbed, which is about 1.8 meters high. They placed the bodies in the cave, cut off their heads and hid them. This way of burial is of course abnormal. Did it involve a kind of demonology or curse? Then these few remaining survivors themselves were soon dying of the disease. So they went somewhere, covered themselves with a kind of Tibetan cloth, then lay

down and died quietly. We discovered this cave and the bodies, and the bodies of the last survivors. You can find the cave. It is over that hill, alongside the riverbed. The bodies are still there, preserved by desert heat."

I went to see the cave later that afternoon, when the sun had crossed and the heat less intense. Sure enough, the headless bodies were piled inside — skin still attached, dried by the heat. The taste of vomit oozed to the bottom of my throat because a pervasive smell of death still lingered in the cave, even though the bodies had been placed here nearly a century ago. Here in Guge's surrounding desert, dryness preserved the odors of death as if it had just occurred yesterday. A moment of horror petrified in the stillness of the desert heat. The question is whether that was a moment of our past, or our future?

Lost Kingdom

"This place could be real or out of a
dream...you do not really know."

Shambhala Sutra

By journeying to this lost kingdom Guge, I had discovered the oracle message encoded in *Shambhala Sutra*: war, environmental destruction and disease arising from human ignorance and short-sighted greed will eventually destroy our world. By uncovering Guge's past, we are walking into our future. But one question remained unanswered: How to change our future?

"Many of my Tibetan friends say this place was Shambhala," explained Han with another puff from his cigarette. "Others visiting from elsewhere say it must have been in Yunnan. This kind of debate is irrelevant. It is hard to say where Shambhala really was. But the kingdom of Guge was locked in a canyon, like a separate realm. And this river follows from mountain snows. So one can say it is quite similar to the place described in *Shambhala Sutra*."

Although Han Xinggang had lived in Ngari for 20 years, he had not read the *Shambhala Sutra*. Therefore he never thought about Guge in this context. "So what else does the sutra say?" he asked curiously.

"*Shambhala Sutra* describes the king of Shambhala residing in a palace on top of a mountain which overlooks the kingdom. From the palace, he can see all the outer rings of our world — mountains, water and fire — which protect the kingdom." I showed him this passage in the sutra text.

Han walked with me to the ruined palace on top of the conical mountain, forming what was once Guge's religious and court center. "Here at the top are the ruins of what we now call the White or Summer Palace. That was where the king and his queens resided. There is a tunnel under the Summer Palace. It was used during war to hide, escape, and store munitions. But now, all those things are gone. It all fits the kind of description of Shambhala Palace you read in the sutra."

The palace sits upon a mountain. Actually, Guge's main ruins — palaces and temples — were built into the sides and on top of this sharp mountain. From here, you can see in all directions, as far as this kingdom stretched.

We looked out across the desert below. Lines of what were once riverbeds could clearly be seen. The kingdom was once entangled within rings of winding rivers stretching through miles of canyon. But now, with global warming, water levels here have dropped and riverbeds are all dry. Beyond the canyon, Han pointed to rings of snow-capped mountains. Beyond the mountains, heat rose from glaring rings of flaming desert.

"Look at the description of how to reach Shambhala," I pointed out in the sutra. "It says you have to cross rings of deserts and snow-capped mountains, and more deserts. Isn't that like traveling to here?" I had been eating dust on the road for weeks. Guge's lost kingdom, locked in this canyon, was like an isolated Shangri-La, inaccessible to the outside.

"That might be why Guge lasted and nobody dared to invade it for so long," Han added, stepping on his burnt out cigarette. "At least not until power within the court had already begun to wane. Actually, critical to Guge's survival and prosperity, was the kingdom's inaccessibility." He reached for another cigarette from the pocket of his blue shirt.

I went on looking for passages in *Shambhala Sutra*. Ge Ming had translated for me entire passages throughout the trip, making notes. "The sutra says on the journey to Shambhala, you must pass 'a mountain called *Gedaigar*', described as 'a black mountain and very frightening'. The sutra claims, 'one of the four Kings of Heaven lives there' and 'it is a place where one can obtain psychic powers'. Have you ever heard of such a mountain near Guge?"

"Actually, there is a black mountain over there," Han pointed at a rounded black shadow protruding from the snow-capped mountains on a distant horizon. "You actually passed it on your way here, but probably did not notice it. That mountain is shaped like a goose head. So if you translate the Tibetan in the

sutra to Chinese, then you get its Chinese name '*Gedaigar*' — literally 'goose head topped' mountain'." Han pulled a lighter from the other pocket and lit his cigarette.

Pensively thinking about everything, he added an afterthought. "As for one of the four Kings of Heaven described, that could refer specifically to the protector spirit associated with that mountain. Just as the sutra describes, that place is quite frightening if you go there. I don't know exactly why. It's just the feeling you get. And there are many caves at the base of this mountain. Monks used to meditate within them to become enlightened or receive certain psychic powers. So in many ways, the description in the sutra can be said to match the place."

I looked through my hand-written notations of translated sutra sections. *Shambhala Sutra* describes, "Many places where people live…it takes months to cross this place of gold, silver, copper, and iron waters."

Han Xinggang's eyes lit. "This is really interesting. Actually, these rivers around Guge once supported huge populations. You can tell by the ruins around here. Moreover, these riverbeds were full of gold. In fact, the main industry of Guge was supplying gold to Kashmir and India. Silver and copper were panned from other rivers of Ngari Prefecture. For instance, near Zhada and Pulan. What else does *Shambhala Sutra* say?"

"The sutra describes the Buddha of Infinite Light in the palace of Shambhala."

Han's eyes widened further. "Certainly by all evidence, the Buddha of Infinite Light was central to religious practice in the court of Guge." He pointed to a mural on the palace wall — fine details almost like an Indian Mogul painting. The king, queens, princes, and even Kashmiri merchants in turbans and curved pointed shoes were paying homage to the Buddha of Infinite Light in the mural. "Actually, nobody has done any research to try and really link all this up to what you have found in *Shambhala Sutra*. But just from a glance at the text, too many

obvious parallels can be made."

I flipped through more hand-written notes. "It describes, 'Cities with many doors and windows in high buildings', something like modern apartment buildings. The sutra goes on to explain how 'each city has populations of over twenty million'. Does that match Guge?"

"Really, Guge fits the sutra's description. The central kingdom was built into the sides of a high, steep mountain. So by appearance, it has many windows and doors at different levels, almost like modern apartment buildings."

"The sutra even explains 'economic conditions were good' in these cities. So this must have once been a rich kingdom, right?"

"All along the Sanquen River to here, there was one vast kingdom locked in this enormous canyon. Aside from the Guge ruins we are in now, there

were many satellite cities of almost the same scale. In fact, people lived in each corner of this vast canyon, which supported a huge population by the standards of that time. Each valley flowed rich with civilization. But most of these potential archeological sites are today inaccessible because there are no roads, or even footpaths. One must travel by horse, then on foot through brush uncut, unmarked. So actually, most of what then constituted the Guge kingdom remains unexplored and undiscovered."

The *Shambhala Sutra* poetically describes the layout of a kingdom stretching like 'an unfolding lotus' from the central palace atop a mountain, from which many sub-kingdoms emanate like petals. Han thought about it pensively for a moment, and agreed that Guge fits this description.

"So far, we have identified at least fourteen major satellite cities around the central one we are sitting in now. But we cannot even begin archeological excavation on most of these sites because of their isolation. So what we really can examine is only here in the central palace and temple complexes." Han turned more pages of the sutra, thinking while smoking. "What we find described in the sutra fits very closely with what we can piece together and imagine once existed here in Guge."

I pointed to another section. "The sutra says that in Shambhala, 'if one family is rich, they give to the poor, so all are equal. There is no fighting, no stealing, no hunger, all are equal but benefiting and rich in this equality.' It describes an almost pure socialist realm. Was Guge such an egalitarian Buddhist kingdom?"

"Of course, everything here in the ruins of Guge is related to Buddhist ideals," Han pointed to the walls. "The murals, the carving and architecture all stem from a set of beliefs, which were the central connecting elements of people who once lived here. These ideals ensured their livelihood and the prosperity they shared."

"So everything here creating this civilization once functioned in the context of a kind of Buddhist egalitarianism? Is that what you are saying, these ideals

underlay the kingdom's prosperity?"

"Just think about it," Han said. "Let me phrase it this way. Nature by virtue of its basic intrinsic self is change. We have spring, summer, autumn and winter. River water freezes in winter and melts in spring. Grass sprouts in spring and dries in winter. As human beings, we must comprehend everything we live with, and everything we are about is subject to constant change. So how should we then understand and interpret humanity's relationship to our natural environment? Respect it? Pray to it? In the past, it was feared."

"But today, it is being desecrated."

"This is a big mistake," Han emphasized. "We are ignoring the order of natural cycles, ignoring what sometimes needs to be feared if it cannot be understood. Our faith in the rewards of capitalist materialism has led to no fear or even belief in the immaterialist powers of nature."

"Then you are saying the spiritual will ultimately overtake the material," I asked, "because it is, in itself, the core element of our natural world?"

"If there is no belief, then one question remains which we cannot answer — where did we come from and where are we going? For all of our empirical science and research, this fundamental question cannot be answered. So it ultimately remains humanity's biggest issue. People seek belief. This cannot change. Only the form of religion or expression of belief can change. But the basic premise of what we are asking does not change."

"So then what are we really asking?"

"What principle do we pursue in our lives? Blind materialism? Does science have all the explanations? Or ultimately is it something else we seek to find, maybe within our own selves?"

"Within our own selves?"

"Our bodies have limitations. The mind requires the body to exist. But are body and mind inseparable? From primitive society to present, this fundamental question has not yet been answered and the search for an answer has not

changed. Only the method or expression of this search has changed."

"So when does this break occur between body and mind?"

"When we have reached limitations over the control of our physical needs," Han exhaled rings of smoke, "that is when we begin to seek the spiritual."

"Physical limitations? What do you mean?"

"Buddhism believes there are three poisons — greed, ignorance, and anger. These are results of the limitations of our bodily desires or physical needs. When we pursue only physical gratification, in the end, we will regret it."

"So in a way, Guge's thousand years of prosperity challenge the very premise of our capitalist ethos that materialism gratifies everything and is the ultimate end onto itself of all things." I stared at murals of Bodhisattvas around staring down at me. "That is what you are trying to get at, right?"

"Think about what ultimately drives humanity," Han asked. "Is it materialism, spirituality or fear? Who are we really? If we do not have at least a little fear of nature's mystery, if we think we are so great that we are the masters of the world, then we will certainly destroy ourselves through war or self-created disease. If one day, we, as human beings, actually allow ourselves to think we are really masters of this world, then this will become our biggest problem. I have spent 20 years in Ngari Prefecture. It is difficult for me to express this clearly, but I feel one thing is certain. The longer I live here, the more I realize as human beings, we do not have that power."

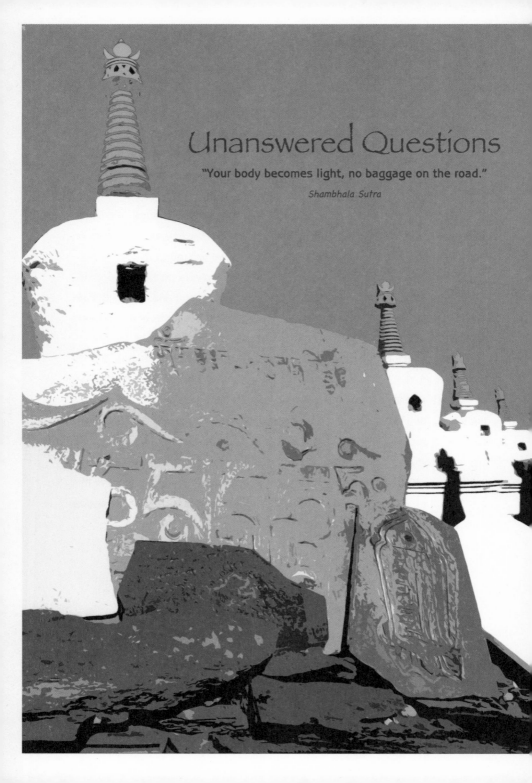

Unanswered Questions

"Your body becomes light, no baggage on the road."

Shambhala Sutra

So where is Shambhala? It all started when a Lhasa antique dealer named La Zha sold me the *Shambhala Sutra*. She claimed a friend gave it to her to sell. By now, I figured out it must have been stolen from the Panchen Lama's palace at Tashilumbo Monastery.

Then at La Zha's shop, I met Renzhen Deki who introduced me to Jokhang Temple's senior monk Nyima Tsering, who then told me to find the Living Buddha Beru Khyentse Rimpoche, who told me to follow the *Shambhala Sutra* on a journey beyond Mount Kailash. Renzhen Deki then introduced me to a driver named Ge Ming. He did not know the way to Shambhala, but could sure drive a jeep.

Following the sutra, it led us to the ruins of the lost kingdom, Guge. There, I met ancient mural specialist Han Xinggang. I asked him if Guge was Shambhala. He could not be sure.

So is Guge really the lost kingdom of Shambhala? Or are its ruins the shadow of our encroaching future?

This journey had become a series of inter-linking individuals. While one connected to another, it seemed the journey was not leading in any specific direction. Or maybe it was?

Frustrated, I asked Han Xinggang for clarification. Does anybody know where Shambhala is? If it is not here in Guge, then where is it? Han pointed to Tuolin Monastery in the nearby valley. He suggested I seek out an 88-year-old monk living there, who just might have the answer, maybe not. Regardless, Han suggested I should ask him anyway. It seemed to me like another link in the chain going nowhere. But having come so far, I went to ask him.

As Ge Ming drove his jeep down the valley toward Tuolin Monastery, he commented in passing, "Yes, I have heard of this monk. He left Tibet in 1958 and went to India. Then sure enough he returned in 1982. He has been staying at Tuolin Monastery ever since."

We entered the monastery. In the late afternoon, it appeared as a series of step-like pagodas, almost resembling pyramids. Some were surrounded with yak horns and skulls. Others swept bare appeared bright red in another setting sun. The style of these pagodas was clearly influenced by India where the great master Atisha came from.

I remembered what Han Xinggang had told me. Atisha had been invited from India by the king of Guge to teach and revive Buddhism in Tibet after it fell into a period of eclipse around the 982 to 1054 A.D. Atisha lived in Guge for years before wandering across Tibet, eventually to the outskirts of Lhasa.

There, Atisha built Dromolakang, the Temple of Twenty-One Taras. Renzhen Deki had taken me to this place along the road to Lhasa, where the Brahmaputra River runs past. The White Tara image, said to be able to speak at Dromolakang, had been brought by Atisha from India first to Guge and then to Dromolakang where Atisha lived out his last days.

Thinking about this, I began to see a connection between everything but was not sure. Were these just coincidences falling upon each other with no actual relationship at all between them? Or is there an invisible network of energy connecting things together that we cannot or choose not to see? Unsure, I chose to dismiss everything as coincidence. Then something clicked in my mind. Renzhen Deki once told me, "In Buddhism, there are no coincidences."

Does everything link up? Interconnecting lives and mindsets among people and places otherwise unconnected should not make sense. But then again, maybe in discovering the Internet, we are only reproducing in a computer function what has always existed in our minds, but, somewhere along the line, we had forgotten how to use. At any rate, I was running out of vacation time and had to get back to my law practice — all those clients waiting and e-mails to be answered. On the other hand, too many questions remained unanswered in my mind.

Determined to find answers to my questions, I took Ge Ming to look for this old monk at Tuolin Monastery. But he did not give me answers. Instead, he left me with more questions.

Ge Ming and I wandered between shadows of red earth-colored, Indian style pagodas of ancient Tuolin Monastery, like in a labyrinth until we merged among shadows. In a doorway stepping into darkness, we followed a staircase to the rooftop of the monastery complex. A small building lay in the corner of the rooftop. We entered the building.

Inside, we found the monk, partly blind and living in a tiny, incense filled yak oil scented room in the small building. Although he could barely see, he could smell the incense. As our presence separated the rising smoke, he became aware of our presence. Rolling his prayer beads between thin, dried fingers, he listened to my question, and shook his head. Finally, he pointed to the sky.

"Actually, Shambhala exists," the old monk replied matter-of-fact. "There are people who have been there. They have even returned to tell us what it is like. But the Panchen Lama can always go there in his dreams at night."

"Why?"

"Actually the text you have been following was written by the Sixth Panchen Lama. But he never visited Guge. Instead, at the invitation of the eighteenth-century Chinese Emperor Qian Long, the Sixth Panchen Lama visited Beijing, where he died. So the *Shambhala Sutra* should be understood as a guide to find the Shambhala within each of us. On the other hand, to mark the journey, he described points and places that clearly exist in Ngari."

"How could he write this guidebook so precisely," I asked, "if he had never visited these places?"

"It was his former incarnation as the Fourth Panchen Lama who visited Guge. All the places described in this text match locations in Ngari Prefecture not because the Sixth Panchen Lama came here, but because he could understand this journey through his dreams as passed on to him by the Fourth Panchen

Lama, who had made this trip."

"Was the trip real or a dream?"

"This is for you to decide. Maybe our world is always somewhere in between dream and reality."

"Is that the underlying message of *Shambhala Sutra*?"

"No, you still have not found it."

"So how can I find it?"

"The only way is to ask his reincarnation."

"You mean the current Eleventh Panchen Lama?"

The old monk nodded.

"Where is he?"

"In Tashilumbo Monastery, sometimes called the Palace of Infinite Light, just

like in the sutra you are carrying."

"That means going to Tashilumbo Monastery in Shigatze to find out, right?"

He nodded again.

"Then I have to backtrack."

He nodded again, "Maybe we all have to backtrack."

"Then this trip is just going around in a big circle. Shigatze is only a day's drive from Lhasa. I've been wasting time."

He shook his head with obvious displeasure at my words, and said nothing.

"But Tashilumbo is where this sutra came from in the first place. So I need to bring it back from where it was taken. Is that the point?"

The monk nodded one last time.

I tried to ask another question.

This time, he did not answer.

Time and Space

"Only by meditation, separating your soul
from your body, can you reach there."

Shambhala Sutra

We left that afternoon, driving back on the route taken toward Shigatze. As the jeep crawled up the narrow steep trail that formed the only road into the canyon of Tulin, I looked back for a moment. Maybe it would be a last glimpse at a desert canyon I had dreamed about throughout a lifetime. Maybe, by leaving, I was just about to enter.

It seemed that in solving the Shambhala riddle, we were just going around in circles. Maybe it had been a nice vacation off the beaten track that should soon end. Maybe it was time to get back to where I had started — the law office, the e-mails, the phone calls, the contracts, the deadlines, the polite conversation to be maintained through dinners with people I never really wanted to talk to in the first place.

On the other hand, maybe the circle might complete a cycle. One situation poses confusion, the other clarity. I was unsure which situation was occurring, circle or cycle.

So maybe confusion creates clarity, I wondered to myself in silence, looking at the red canyon walls passing outside our jeep window. Opening the window, red dust poured inside the jeep, filling it.

We approached a small, tented community. It was just another rest stop on the road from Ngari to Shigatze. In fact, there was only one road. We stopped to clean out the jeep. Dogs barked. A Kham lady with big chunks of turquoise in her hair churned yak butter. Entering the tent, we saw trays of dried meat lying on the table. Ge Ming picked up one. Drawing a knife from his belt, he began cutting pieces, eating it as an afternoon snack.

Here of all places, I met Zouge Rimpoche. He was a Living Buddha of the Jonangpa, an esoteric branch of Tibetan Buddhism, dedicated to Shambhala practice. So I asked him about Shambhala. He said many people were now looking but could not find it. Maybe some are looking too hard. Maybe some are not looking hard enough.

I didn't think this was an answer. Anxious to get back on the road, I was looking at my watch. He told me not to look at it so seriously. Time is only a gimmick. Our watches are just a street fashion statement. Actually, they have nothing to do with time.

The Kham lady had just finished churning the yak butter. She mixed it with black tea. She poured two cups of yak butter tea and placed them on the wooden table that seemed to fill this tent pushing us to its edges. We both sipped tea. I stopped looking at my watch and began to listen.

Zouge Rimpoche explained how the Kalachakra, or the Wheel of Time, is the basis of Shambhala philosophy. He retrieved a *thanka* from a backpack kept beside him. In the center, a blue man embraced a yellow woman. He explained the imagery has nothing to do with sex, and asked me not to think of it that way. "This represents the merging of compassion and wisdom," explained Zouge Rimpoche.

I stared at the *thanka*. The embracing couple seemed to have many heads, with third eyes facing in all directions and many arms, each with a weapon — swords, lassos — and lots of other things I could not identify clearly but had seen painted on similar murals in the ruins of Guge. Together, the embracing figures stood upon two smaller figures beneath their feet, each embracing a miniature consort of their own.

"Those are not people being crushed beneath their feet but demons representing greed and short-sighted ignorance, which now plague our society," Zouge interpreted the imagery. "These elements only breed frustration and in turn, sorrow. By merging compassion with wisdom, the Kalachakra can crush greed and ignorance."

It sounded so complicated, yet also simple. "So how does this relate to finding Shambhala?"

"If each person can achieve this intention, crushing greed and ignorance by

merging compassion with wisdom, then positive energy can overcome negative. The planetary movements can finally be re-aligned. Our seasons can once again be set clear. Each of us can find Shambhala."

He explained that the Shambhala *mandala* is core to the Kalachakra teachings. It established a realm to be crossed. Within the realm are elements of wind, fire, water and earth. The Kalachakra deity resides within the Palace of Infinite Light that rises upon Mount Meru, in the center of Shambhala *mandala*. Maybe the center of our universe is embodied in our earth, which is really just a realm, within each of our own bodies and mind. Maybe our minds are as unlimited as the universe if we release them.

"We drove through wind, flaming desert, past lakes and through rivers, to the sacred mountain Kailash, then on to the lost kingdom of Guge." I asked, still smothered in red dust, "So in actuality, we've been driving through a Shambhala *mandala*, right?"

"Maybe everyday you are journeying through a Shambhala *mandala*," he smiled. "You do not necessarily have to come to Tibet to do this. The question is, can you go through each of its rings to reach the center and can you do this every day?"

"But what does that have to do with finding Shambhala?"

"When you can do it every day, the question becomes 'can you do it many times a day'. When you can, the question becomes 'can you do it every moment'. When you can, maybe you will have already arrived at Shambhala without knowing it."

"How does all of this fit in with Buddhist teachings?" I asked incredulously, trying to put the pieces together again.

"The Buddha Shakyamuni, just before death, took on the form of the deity Kalachakra and preached this doctrine at a place called Dhanyakataka in southern India near where Amaravati is today," Zouge Rimpoche explained. "Among the audience was Suchandra, the first king of Shambhala. He took this teaching back to his kingdom, built the Shambhala *mandala* in three-dimensional form, and taught his people how to use their minds to harness positive energy and find future peace."

"Was Guge the lost kingdom of Shambhala or not?" I still insisted on an exact answer to this whole thing if it was going to make any sense. "The sutra says Shambhala is north. So that part makes sense. You said that place is in southern India. This makes Guge north of that place. The sutra also says there is a place south of Shambhala called Malaya. They must have meant the Himalayas. I am not an archeologist or anything, but, well, it sounds pretty close to me. What do you think?"

Zouge Rimpoche said nothing. He just sat there, seemingly staring at something. But nothing was there. I realized he was not interested in my piecing the puzzle together. Actually, while busily fitting together the pieces, I was missing the whole point, while he was trying to explain a picture of how the puzzle should look when it was complete. He was not interested in archeological expedition discoveries. His interest in the past was that it determined our present position in relation to the universe. His interest in our present was that it would lead us into the future.

He began again, continuing to explain slowly. "Manjushrikirti founded the lineage by uniting all Shambhala factions into one 'diamond caste'. His descendants were given the title 'Kulika Rikden', which means 'Holder of the Castes'."

"So there was a line of kings, just like Guge?"

"There were 25 kings of Shambhala who were entrusted to preserve the Kalachakra teachings. Each king ruled for a reign of 100 years. The Panchen Lamas have been traditionally considered to be manifestations of the Shambhala kings on earth because Panchen Lama is believed to be the reincarnation of Manjushrikirti."

"Is it true, to find Shambhala, I must go to see him?"

"You can try to go to Tashilumbo Monastery. It is in the holy city of Shigatze in central Tibet, not far from where we are now, only a few hundred more kilometers.

156

Tashilumbo is the palace where the Panchen Lamas reside. There you will come to understand how all of this connects. Just remember one thing, the Wheel of Time is also a calendar. Using the calendar, we can begin the countdown."

"Countdown? What are we counting?"

"Time. It is always with us even if it is never there. So we seek to define the indefinable."

"Can it be defined?"

"No."

"Then how do we define it?"

"We don't. Rather, we shatter its definition. This way, we can overcome time."

"Then what about space?"

"It too becomes an illusion."

"How is that?"

"Space exists as figments of a moment locked in the contraption of time."

"So how do you unlock the moment?"

"By shattering the contraption."

"Which means time?"

"Exactly."

"If time does not exist, then how much of it do we really have left?"

"We don't."

"Things are that bad?"

"No," Zouge Rimpoche smiled. "Not really."

"Why are you optimistic?"

"Because time and space, as concepts, were never there to begin with. We only made them up."

"So when one's mind realizes this…"

"Then you have shattered time and space."

"Then what?"

"You are no longer living in the box."

Panchen Lama

"Tibetan monks who meditated very high have been able
to go within one or two years...yes, they can go to Shambhala...
When the Panchen Lama sleeps he goes there every night."

Shambhala Sutra

It was late in the afternoon, but the gates of Tashilumbo Monastery had not yet closed. So I entered. The monastery seemed tucked into the side of a softly rounding mountain. Tibetans say it is cradled between the breasts of White Tara, embraced in her arms. I asked why. The monks did not answer. They just explained that the Tenth Panchen Lama always carried with him a small but ancient figure of White Tara. I thought about it. Atisha also carried such a White Tara figure. I had been blessed with it by a monk at the Tara Temple at Dromolakang, which Renzhen Deki took me to outside Lhasa before beginning this journey.

A monk named Dor Cheng met me at the entrance of Tashilumbo. He knew why I had come. At this point in a journey, words become unnecessary because the intention had already become clear. He could read the intention between lines of red dust, which had now caked every inch of my skin.

The colors of Tashilumbo are orange. Upon orange walls within are massive murals. They are huge versions of the tiny mural painted on a corner wall at Jokhang, depicting the epic war between armies of Shambhala and Kali. But here, the enormity of these murals places this epic struggle in the forefront of questioning. As positive forces of peace and social harmony struggle against negative forces of war and intolerance, who will win?

The upper portion of these murals depicts Shambhala as a dimension shaped like an eight-petaled lotus surrounded by two rings of snow-covered mountains, exactly as described in the sutra. The king of Shambhala residing in a palace of infinite light teaches his philosophy at the center of a lotus shaped world.

Armies of destruction enter from the west. They are set to conquer our world and unify it under an empire driven by values of greed and materialism. While these are only illusions of happiness, they are covered under an umbrella of ideology. Such an ideology appears supreme only because of its intolerance.

According to the story, desires of capital accumulation and conspicuous consumption only breed frustration followed by anger. Everything begins to fall apart. Ignorance arises from distorted values, failed priorities and dysfunctional lifestyles, leading forces of Kali to rise in the self-created chaos and embark on unilateral conquests. In the end, such wars will only destroy our world.

From the fingers of the Shambhala king spins a wheel representing a thorough turning of events. Once again, the question resounded in my mind against the orange walls. Doesn't the word 'revolution' mean a complete 360-degree turning of a wheel?

Rudrachakrin, the future king of Shambhala, emerges from the kingdom of peace together with his general Hanumanda riding a powerful steed and swinging a massive spear. Winged elephants and armies of Shambhala, supported by flying Dakinis on clouds hurling wheels of fire, ultimately crush forces of negativity and greed.

But who are the soldiers of Shambhala? An ancient Chinese song echoes, "I will go into the jungle for justice, and the rain will be my drink." It seems that these days, this is the road many have chosen to take.

I wondered about all this, and asked Dor Cheng. "There are 25 Shambhala kings," he explained in a soft voice. "They are represented here by 24 meditating monks and the Panchen Lama himself. Shambhala is a lotus-like realm with eight petals separating different lands. The Shambhala King is Panchen Lama. Everyday, the focus of his meditation is for world peace. We can attain peace by avoiding war. We can avoid war by avoiding each wrong step through correct action and positive intention in everything we do each day."

Dor Cheng then led me into a long hallway. Sutras were stacked on a stretch of wall alongside the corridor. Through wafting incense and triangles of light sifting through small half-triangle windows, we walked down the corridor. Afternoon

light tinted purple stretched across the corridor's smooth yak oiled surface, illuminating the orange walls stacked with sutras on each side.

"You will not be needing this anymore," Dor Cheng pointed to the black box under my arm, which had carried me on this journey. "You are now in the Palace of Infinite Light," he explained. "The *Shambhala Sutra* has brought you here to Tashilumbo Monastery. You are about to meet the Panchen Lama. He is the king of Shambhala. You should not be needing this sutra anymore." He stopped in the corridor before a monk who was dusting off the sutras stacked against the wall. "Please return the *Shambhala Sutra* to where it belongs. We have been missing it for some time."

I was shocked. The monk turned around from dusting off the sutras and stepped toward me. Taking the black yak skin box from my hands, he abruptly turned around and returned the *Shambhala Sutra* to its place in a shelf along the wall. The sutra had returned to where it belonged. It had come full circle.

Dor Cheng then led me into a vast hallway lit with yak butter candles. The whole audience room was filled with the color orange. At the far end of the room sat His Holiness the Eleventh Panchen Lama, who has hardly been seen by the outside world. I prostrated before him three times. He nodded for me to sit at one side of the room across from a row of monks on the other side. Low Tibetan tables with fruit laid upon them were spread before us. A monk poured yak butter tea. Another attending monk whispered in my ear. "You may ask His Holiness what you wish to know."

"I have been searching for Shambhala," I explained, "what we westerners now understand as Shangri-La. I have traveled throughout Tibet across mountains and deserts, but still cannot find it. I came here today to ask one question. Can you please tell me where Shambhala is?"

He smiled and folded both hands together. "Originally, the concept of Shambhala came from India, where the first Buddha Shakyamuni was born," he explained matter-of-factly. "Many people thought of it as a dimension. In Tibetan history, many famous Buddhist scholars, including my predecessors — the First, Sixth and Ninth Panchen Lama — spoke and wrote about Shambhala, describing the location as a harmonious place."

"If it is such a harmonious place, in each person's own search," I asked, "then how can we reach Shambhala?"

"It is hard to say if each person can reach Shambhala," he smiled again. "It depends on determination and study. If you study hard enough, and continue to learn and think positively, you can reach there."

Things cannot be so straightforward, I thought, just think positively and you can reach there? I had already crossed deserts and mountains but was nowhere near the place. There had to be another answer. I thought about what Nyima Tsering had said and asked the question a different way. "The world faces many problems — war, disease, environmental desecration — often brought about by short-sighted greed and materialism. If Shambhala is the 'future' ideal, how will Shambhala help us?"

"In the Shambhala dimension, the King of Shambhala must use positive energy to destroy evil caused by negative energy. By this, the environment can be protected, people can live longer, Buddhist ideals will flourish, and there will be peace and harmony among humanity."

Clearly, his point was positive intention. It can overcome negative as energy forces. But if that is the case, then why so much war? Seemingly negative thinking people had already overtaken the positive in our current world order. "So then for peace on earth," I asked. "What should we do?"

"Firstly, use compassion to help others, even at your own loss. Then there will be peace. If you are selfish and achieve for yourself at a loss to others, then the world will have no peace."

The Eleventh Panchen Lama was only 15 years old. His answer was pure, but cut to the point. He continued the thought, "Many countries spend much money to buy arms and weapons of mass destruction. By doing so, the country will

gain power for their country, but it will bring harm to the world. This expense is very large and tremendous. If these countries use this money to help the less developed countries and nationalities, if this money went to disabled people and students and for buying medical facilities and promoting medical research, then there will be peace."

"Today, I have learned a lot from Your Holiness. As I leave here and go back to where I come from, is there any message you want me to take to the outside world?"

"First, I wish the world may enjoy peace and that people love and respect each other. May there be tolerance among different religions and beliefs. Secondly, I wish that Tibetan people here and those living abroad will love their country

and hometown. I wish they will put their efforts into economic development in order to raise living standards and develop their hometown. In the end, I will pray in English for the world — I pray for peace in the world. May Buddha bless human beings."

These were the words of a 15-year-old reincarnated *lama* or 'Living Buddha,' spoken from the vast and distant Tashilumbo Monastery in isolated Shigatze. But maybe from his vantage point, on the rooftop of our world, he could see clearly what was happening.

As I left Tashilumbo Monastery, I thought about the *Shambhala Sutra* I had carried across western Tibet, eventually returning it to Tashilumbo Monastery. The sutra prophesizes how a Panchen Lama will be reborn. He will harness positive energy to defeat the negative forces sent from the west. A blood-red sun will rise in the east, heralding a new harmonious age called Shambhala.

Maybe all of this written in the sutra and depicted in the murals of Tashilumbo is just a dream. But maybe the struggle is real and already upon us. Should

we stop fighting for a future of peace and harmony for our children, even if its realization is only a dream?

They tell you not to dream. Stock and oil prices are reality. Dreaming during the daytime can be dangerous. If it was not reported on major western television networks, then it did not happen, right? So why bother dreaming?

The Homeland Security and CIA are everywhere and see everything, right? But despite their sophisticated technological gadgetry, can they see into our dreams?

Is it not right to dream for peace and harmony? The short-term interests of a greed-dominated materialist-driven minority adhering to an ideology of self-righteousness will destroy our world and environment. This is not just an oracle written in a lost Tibetan prayer book, but already an advanced process.

Can we stop the process?

Our Future

"There is no disease, if one family is rich they give to the poor, so all are equal. There is no fighting, no stealing, no hunger, all are equal but benefiting and rich in this equality."

Shambhala Sutra

Everyone in Lhasa knew we had just returned from Ngari Prefecture. All they had to do was look at our jeep, covered with red dust. All they had to do was look at me. I was covered with red dust too.

Upon returning to Lhasa, I checked into a small guesthouse. I dumped my bags and camera in the room, and almost on impulse, went straight to Jokhang Temple. Before Jokhang's vast yak butter oiled doors, Tibetan pilgrims prostrated stretching their entire bodies upon the stone slab plaza, faces to the earth, hands clasped and stretched toward the door. It was already early evening. I entered the door.

Senior monk Nyima Tsering was where we last met over a month ago before I departed for Ngari Prefecture and got on the road to Shambhala, by following the *Shambhala Sutra*. Standing up, he invited me to join him for dinner, leading the way across stone slabs laid centuries ago in the courtyard, into a large room with low tables, which was empty. Most of the monks had already eaten and retired to study sutra. He asked me to sit at one of the tables and went to a large pot where a monk scooped out two bowls of noodles with pieces of yak meat. After crossing through Ngari, I was now used to eating yak.

I began to tell him about the trip — meeting the Panchen Lama, returning *Shambhala Sutra* to Tashilumbo Monastery — and what I had found, especially at Guge, an exquisite Buddhist egalitarian civilization that was wiped out by war precipitated by intrusion of western religious fundamentalism. The war had been followed by disease. I was trying to make some sense out of the experience, and to put it in perspective.

Explaining to Nyima Tsering the route I had taken, following *Shambhala Sutra* literally like a guidebook, I said, "It led west and a little north through Ngari Prefecture."

"This is the most remote, isolated part of Tibet where many ancient things are still preserved in their purity," said Nyima Tsering. "The murals on the temple walls of Guge's ruins are untouched as they were painted maybe 900 years ago."

"You would have seen in these murals images of powerful Yidams, like Kalachakra or Yamantaka", Nyima Tsering explained. "They are often depicted as embracing consorts, representing the merging of compassion with wisdom, to create emptiness and realize the non-duality of our existence. They are standing upon figures of angry people being crushed beneath their feet. Actually, those figures under their feet are not supposed to be people, but symbols of negative forces. What the Yidams are really crushing is our own ignorance, greed and anger. By crushing these beneath us, we can rise to higher aspirations."

"Then why do these Yidams look so furious? They themselves appear angry."

"Did you look carefully at the murals?" Nyima Tsering pressed. "Many of

these Buddhist Yidams have multiple arms, with each one grasping a different weapon. These are not weapons to be used by a powerful nation to liberate, conquer, take over, take advantage of, or invade a small nation. No. These are weapons of knowledge and compassion to be used to crush ignorance, greed and anger within our own selves."

"So they are not to fight others," I asked incredulously. "But to fight the demons in ourselves?"

Having just finished our bowls of yak noodles, Nyima Tsering led me out from the monks' mess hall back across the courtyard ascending a long wooden stair ladder to the second floor, down a corridor toward the back of Jokhang where the monks' quarters were. He reminded me to duck my head through the low ancient doorway and led me into a small but spacious room delicately lit by yak butter candles. The first thing he did was pour a cup of yak butter tea and hand it to me. Then, after I took a sip, he began to answer my question.

"Ultimately, this is the epic war for Shambhala," Nyima Tsering said, his shadow flickering against the wall as a yak butter candle dissipated under the weight of its own flame on the table before us. "The real enemy is within. It is our own selves. By crushing the enemy within, we can achieve peace. Real wisdom is to respect other people's paths, not to judge them or tell them what to do. Regardless of whether you are a big nation or a small one, respect the space others live in. You cannot conquer that space occupied by others or try to step into it and force your ways upon them."

"But it seems in our world today that certain nations are determined to force others to be like them, to accept their economic models and political theology," I said, taking another sip of tea. The candle flickered, illuminating part of the orange wall behind him. The rest of the room was already melting into shadows.

"If each person takes care to find their correct path, and then follows it well themselves without interfering with others, then we can collectively find a road to peace," explained Nyima Tsering. "Only by bringing about peace can we usher in the era of Shambhala."

"So does much of the problem lie in forcing a single ideology, both political and economic, on others?"

"This so-called 'globalization' dogma has actually become a key problem. Smashing your methodology onto the heads of others and telling them to accept it is not a realistic solution. They will resist and even counter it. That is the problem the world is facing today. In some respects, 'globalization' as a political-economic ideology and goal onto itself is impracticable," Nyima Tsering pointed out.

"Remember, each person's ability to accept something is limited by their conditionality and circumstances," Nyima Tsering explained, raising a finger in the prevailing darkness. "So you cannot force things upon people based on your individual experience, or what you think is right for them because it may have worked for you. It is impossible."

"So you are not a melting-pot advocate? Don't your ideas run counter to the formulas of certain economic and financial institutions such as the International Monetary Fund and World Bank? You are really talking about something bigger than just Buddhist philosophy."

"Globalization of technology, science and medical treatment is what true globalization should be about," Nyima Tsering explained, clarifying his position. "But so-called 'globalization' advocates insist on one methodology for everything. By insisting on a cookie cutter application to solving global problems, they will find themselves in conflict with humanity's natural diversity."

For the first time, it became crystal clear that here at the top of the Himalayan plateau, monks are discussing ideas arguably among the most progressive in the world. Hence, in Tibet's most revered monastery, one monk's voice is prepared to challenge the very fundamentals of a global structure driving toward its own self-demise.

"The survival of every species arises from diversity. Otherwise, why would we advocate 84,000 paths in Buddhism if only one path was exclusive and correct? If there is really a fast track, then everyone will jump onto it. But they are not doing so; so ask yourself, why? Each person, each culture, and in turn, each nation has their own differences. You and I are not the same. So the methods and paths we must choose to take in this life cannot be the same. The greater diversity in our world process, the better for everyone."

"So you are advocating not just ethnic, but economic, financial, or even political diversity?"

"In Buddhism, we say there are 84,000 doors you can enter and roads which can be followed. Each is correct. Diversity is good. Just try to accept others for what they are."

"Maybe the structure of our current world order runs counter to the natural diversity of humanity. So the real question is whether philosophies contained in a Buddhist approach toward encouraging diversity may be applied to economics and finance, even politics and political systems?"

"Yes, because Buddhism does not present a religion in the western context or understanding as such, but rather a framework of ideas built around principles of compassion and rational knowledge. These are teachings for better living. They are frameworks or tools to be applied by the individuals, not just for themselves, but for others as well."

"Then Buddhism is not really religion, but rather a philosophy of life and living? Is that what you are saying?" Yak butter candles were burning low. Tea was dissipating.

"The first Buddha did not invent a religion. Rather, he discovered the interconnectivity of our universe with our selves. The results of each person's life are derived from their own individual action. We can change the outcome of many things by our action. We always have this option, the power to use positive energy to overcome the negative. It is only a question of whether we

wish to. That is a final question of intention."

I took another sip of yak butter tea. The room had now faded into shadow as the light descended deeper into the brass candlestick holding yak butter. I thought about what Nyima Tsering said. In a way, a monk sitting on the top of the world was shattering the assumptions upon which it has been built, or rather upon which we have been conditioned to believe it should be built.

I thought more, sipping yak butter tea. Didn't Adam Smith tell us that greed is good? At least, that is what the textbooks say, as long as everybody is greedier than everyone else, the stock markets will continue to go up. The 'invisible hand' will rule. You don't have to worry about anything else because big brother will take care of it all for you. So part of the success of our greed-based material invisible hand driven society is to keep you from questioning any of those things, which you are expected to take for granted. Remember 'all the news which is fit to print' is in the *New York Times*. So if they don't publish it, then it didn't happen, right?

"Think about our current world order," Nyima Tsering perked up at the question.

"A huge amount of oil is used to support this system of self-perpetuated greed and branded shareholder's value. What for? Think about it. A huge chunk of our world economy is spent chasing illusions."

"What do you mean?" I asked, sipping a cup of tea that was half empty. "What illusions?"

Nyima Tsering leaned forward and filled the cup.

"Brand conspicuous consumption creates values that drive consumers to blindly purchase these products. Consumers may work hard for their money. They save, sometimes for a lifetime, and in the end, just spend it on consumer brands — items with no intrinsic value other than their brand names. But because the media tells consumers they must have this as social identification, they stress themselves to earn the money to purchase them. People borrow for a lifetime, leveraging everything they own, just to wear one of these labels. It is just a badge. Actually, it is just a waste of time and life. These are just empty names. They have nothing, just a bubble. Meaningless."

"So you are blaming the multinationals for misguiding people through their advertising? What about shareholder's value? The world turns on this."

"Think about the substance," Nyima Tsering cautioned, touching the Tibetan rug upon which he sat. "If you break the bubble, is there real productivity underneath that shareholder's value benefiting people? Look at this carpet. This is real, woven by Tibetan women using lots of time, care and feeling. The fur is real yak. Unlike fashion, it can weather all four seasons and is soft to sit upon. So do we need all this synthetic and plastic just because it has some designer's name upon it?"

"So you are questioning the conspicuous consumption values driving our society, or society's underlying materialism?"

"Too much material wealth is being spent on war and mutual deceit to conquer others. If governments take values of spirituality as a moral basis of action and combine them with rational materialism, then we will all be moving in the direction of a real Shambhala."

"But this whole system accounts for a vast chunk of our world economy. So you are saying through the ideals of Shambhala, there can be a new world economic order?"

"Remember, spirituality can overcome materialism. Our twenty-first century has now already shown us that materialism alone does not bring human happiness. Using knowledge and rational thought as its basis, I believe we can contribute to creating a new world economic order. But under our current system structured around notions of invisible hand greed, the wasting of resources to chase illusionary brand images, the result has only been more wars of destruction to control those resources, in turn accumulating more negative karma."

"Where is this going?"

"The result will be our own self-destruction," explained Nyima Tsering.

"It is time we opened forums to discuss a new set of ideas, and new economic

models using compassion and knowledge as their basis, not the invisible hand of short-sighted greed. If rationality and compassion can become the underlying spirit of a new system, then the economy will be healthy."

"Then in a way, the problem with our world system today is that one model is being rammed down the throats of everyone?"

"One model is not correct," Nyima Tsering stressed. "We can select many different kinds of models, economic and political. Old systems can be merged with new. We can shatter the box and rigidity of what we have created when it becomes blind repetition and create something else using the pieces."

The candle had dissipated. Incense had burned to the bottom of each bowl. The room was enveloped in darkness. Nyima Tsering's voice could still be heard.

He whispered softly but deliberately, his words echoing against the thick, orange adobe walls of his room. "Earth can become Shambhala. Remember Shambhala does not need to be found somewhere else. It can be created by each of us, right here, right now, at any time. There is only one question: whether we want to or not."

Story End

"Without clarity of mind, you cannot go there."

Shambhala Sutra

Leaving Jokhang Temple, Nyima Tsering guided me across the rooftop. Purple darkness had already covered the sky. I realized we had talked late into the night. Jokhang, normally thronged with pilgrims and tourists, had become so silent one could almost hear the echo of clouds moving over the moon above.

I could barely follow Nyima Tsering across the rooftop because it was so dark. The autumn air felt as if it was about to rain. He quickly led me downstairs, waving goodbye as I slipped through the thick yak oil soaked red doors of Jokhang Temple. They slammed behind me. I stood alone in the plaza before Jokhang. There was nobody there. The presence of absolutely nobody crept around me. It was the feeling of being alone.

I wandered clockwise along the pilgrimage route, circumambulating Jokhang. It was after midnight and Barkor Street was empty. The market stalls were only wooden boards waiting to be repossessed by sellers at dawn. There was nobody in the street. A chill rain drizzled and clouds began covering the full moon.

The streets became dark. I could hear the energy of pilgrims praying and prostrating, but nobody was there. It was already too late. Their total commitment filled the space between echoes of prayers said throughout the day. It could still be felt, even when they were sleeping. Their devotion to an ideal still resounded on the yak butter smoothed stones. The faint echo of mantra already recited filled the darkness which was unfulfilled because it had not yet seen moonlight. The moon could not be seen anymore. Then it rained.

As I rounded the back bend of Barkor into the street behind Jokhang, I could see a light was still on in that teahouse on the second floor of an old yellow stone building on a corner of the Barkor. There were no other lights lit along the street.

I could barely see Renzhen Deki's figure, a silhouette wearing a turquoise necklace over a torn shirt, picking up teacups. Someone had spilled tea, the cup had been left sideways.

The rain now turned to ice. The summer had clearly gone. It was autumn. Wrapping a red dust starched scarf across my face, I walked faster over old cobblestones toward her teahouse. Wind blew at the entrance.

Passing between thick walls, I found it was warm inside. Within moments, smells of yak butter and Tibetan incense filled my senses. I walked upstairs and sat down at one of her large wooden tables, which were as thick as a temple door.

She sat down across from me. "After ten days, I did not think you were coming back."

"The trip took longer than I thought. But see, I came back."

She smiled, said nothing and wiped a Tibetan teacup. She then poured yak butter tea. It tasted fresh and hot.

I drank it quickly, fighting the cold just felt outside.

She poured another cup — it warmed against the chill.

"Did you find it?" she asked.

"Find what?"

"Shambhala, of course. Wasn't that what you went looking for?"

"Yes, maybe, maybe not," I stuttered. "Actually, I am really not all that sure, but I went and came back, and maybe now have I some idea where it is."

Sure enough, I had come back to her teahouse in Barkor Market, where in a way, the trip had sort of begun. The journey was not really a long straight line going somewhere else as anticipated after all. Rather, it was a full circle.

Once again, I thought, isn't a revolution just another way of describing a 360-degree turning of the wheel? I suddenly realized before the journey started, Renzhen Deki had pointed in all the directions at once without saying so. But the paths all led back to the same place.

"We are burdened by our past and fear our future," she said with a forlorn

sigh lost in the waft of incense. It rose to the ceiling of her teahouse, staining it black. Her silver bracelets cling-clanged while filling the teacup to its brim. She then thought pensively, placing the teacup before me again with a sense of caution seeming like apprehension. "But if we concentrate on the present, then there is neither burden nor fear. For all which follows from the present is the future. The result of this depends on intention. Everyone's intention starts now."

I had been doubtful but now was certain Renzhen Deki must have known the result of my trip even before it began. Was she psychic or just intuitive? I hesitated to ask, suspecting she would forget to tell me because something else was on her mind. Actually, she had forgotten those things but was trying to remember something else. By remembering, she forgot everything else.

Others guessed she was absentminded. Maybe she was actually thinking all the time without letting anyone know. Maybe it was all that mantra reciting or just a state of momentary confusion between tea orders. Now the yak butter tea went to that table, Indian Masala Chai to the other one, and yes, that sweet Tibetan milk tea, this order goes to that table over there.

"Oh no, they have already left without paying the bill," she exclaimed with disappointment, soon dissipating into acceptance. She shrugged. "These things always seem to happen to me."

"Of course, they have been waiting while you were talking with me," I pointed out.

She didn't really want to hear this and just shrugged both shoulders again. Time was not a necessary part of her life. She believed with conviction that people stumbled upon her teahouse to drink tea and whittle away an entire afternoon or an evening, not to be held hostage to a schedule or time.

Time! It drifted with the clouds above in a starry sky after midnight when she sat on the rooftop of her teahouse, after the guests had all left, staring at the universe unfolding in the purple Lhasa sky above. This was the best time.

It was quiet. She could recite her favorite mantra with slow deliberation, shifting ivory prayer beads between both fingers without ever becoming too involved with the passing of each.

I was just warming from tea against the chill outside those thick adobe walls of her teahouse when Renzhen Deki shattered my thoughts again. "Today must end here, because we are not sure what tomorrow will bring." I was just beginning to enjoy calm thoughts after a long, cold, dust-fulfilled trip and did not understand what she meant. "Don't speak," she intercepted my thought, with eyebrows arched into half a warning, as if the bridge might just collapse.

"Why?" I asked. "What's running through your head now?"

"What you wish to say I already heard," she said with certainty. "What you wish to tell I already know. You said it without saying it. You thought it without thinking it. Because of this reason, I know what you felt before you could rationalize it. If you try to articulate it, it will disappear. If you grasp the thought, it may be forgotten. If you write it down, I won't read it. If you try to take it with you, I cannot let you go. If you leave it behind, I will let you leave. But if you stay a while, I will tell you a story."

"A story?"

"Would you like to hear my story? It will just take a moment."

"Ok. Then tell me your story."

She opened that small book she always kept on the table before her and began to turn the pages with long fingernails painted like a 60s flower child's. She came to a line and began to read, eyes shifting down upon the page with a concentration that seemed complete. "Many centuries ago, His Holiness the Sixth Dalai Lama used to sneak out of the Potala Palace at night. He was a romantic who loved to drink and sing. He wrote the most beautiful poetry in Tibet and we sing his poetry in songs today. Then one night, he came to this teahouse, the house we are in right now, my teahouse. He began to write poetry and sing. Then suddenly from behind a curtain, he caught the glimpse of a beautiful young girl whose charm entranced him at first sight. Convinced he had seen the Bodhisattva, White Tara, he returned to this teahouse almost every night, very late, searching for her. She never appeared again." Renzhen Deki sighed and looked up.

"Then what happened?"

"He wandered off and never returned to the Potala Palace. He died looking for her."

"That's a sad story. Maybe it is a tragedy."

"Maybe it is not. Sometimes, finding what you are looking for is not as important as searching for it. What do you think?"

"I think maybe you think you are that White Tara he was looking for. Now tell me the truth. Are you a Bodhisattva in disguise?"

Behaving as one might think a Bodhisattva would, but can never really be sure, unless you have met one, Renzhen Deki just smiled a bit, but remembered not to laugh. Then slowly and deliberately, opening the book again, she began re-reading her story. I thought this was strange, because now this was the third time I was hearing it. Then again, sometimes, some things just need repeating. Maybe I had not been listening carefully enough. She reminded me, I had already crossed the desert.